Annette's People

The Metis

David C. Rempel
Laurence Anderson

Plains Publishing Inc.

BANFF TRAIL EL

Cataloguing in Publication Data
Rempel, David C., 1927 -
Annette's people: the Metis
ISBN 0-920985-22-X
1. Metis - Canada, Western, Juvenile literature.* I. Anderson, Laurence. II. Title.
FC109.R44 1987   j971.2'00497   C87-091263-1
E99.M693R44 1987

Plains Publishing Inc.
10316 - 121 Street,
Edmonton, Alberta
Canada T5N 1K8

The Song My Paddle Sings, by Pauline Johnston (pp. 73 - 77) copyright Thomas Nelson & Sons Ltd.

Original Illustrations by:
Wendy Kershaw, Willie Big Bull, Henry Standing Alone

Typesetting and Design:
Pièce de Résistance Ltd.

Colour Separations and Stripping:
Color Graphics Alberta Ltd.

Printing and Binding:
Friesen Printers Ltd.

Printed and Bound in Canada

Acknowledgements

The manuscript for this book was developed under the auspices of Alberta Education through monies provided by the Native Education Project. The project is under the direction of Dr. Ralph Sabey, Merv Kowalchuk and Pearl Calahasen.

This book was produced as a result of a cooperative effort involving:

Medicine Hat Metis Local (M.H.M.L.) #89
Medicine Hat School District (M.H.S.D.) #76
Medicine Hat Catholic Board of Education (M.H.C.B.E.) #21

The mutualistic model employed in developing this book involved the efforts of many people. The Publisher would like to gratefully acknowledge the contributions of the following individuals and organizations:

Dr. Laurence Anderson, Associate Writer; M.H.M.L. #89;
Mr. Cal Annis, Lethbridge Regional Office, Alberta Education;
Mr. Harvey Cardinal, Steering Committee; M.H.M.L. #89;
Mr. Pat Glashan, Steering Committee Secretary; M.H.C.B.E. #21;
Mr. Cal Hauserman, Teacher, M.H.S.D. #76;
Mrs. Isabelle Henderson, Working Committee; Lethbridge
    Regional Office, Alberta Education;
Mr. David Leahy, Working Committee; Teacher, M.H.C.B.E. #21;
Mr. Les Omotani, Steering Committee Chairperson;
    M.H.S.D. #76;
Mr. Terry Quesnelle, Steering Committee; M.H.M.L. #89;
Ms. Joyce Quilty, Social Studies Consultant, Lethbridge
    School District #51;
Mr. David Rempel, Principal Writer; M.H.S.D. #76;
Dr. Ken Sauer, Steering Committee; Superintendent, M.H.S.D. #76;
Mrs. Marcella Smith, Working Committee; Teacher, M.H.S.D. #76;
Mr. Keith Wagner, Associate Director of Curriculum,
    Alberta Education.

Native Validation: Medicine Hat Metis Local #89.

Contents

About this Book

This book tells a story about Annette McKay. At the beginning of the story Annette learns that she is **Metis**. That means that some of Annette's **ancestors** were **Indians** while others were **European**. Annette wants to learn more about her Metis **heritage**.

How would you go about finding out where your family came from? By reading Annette's story you will see how she found out about her own family **history**. Annette learns how the Metis people lived in the past and how Metis people have **adapted** to change over the years. Learning about the past helps Annette to learn more about herself.

Annette lives with her brother Duncan and her Mom and Dad. The McKay family lives in the City of *Medicine Hat* in southeastern Alberta. In the story Annette and her family travel to many different places such as *Edmonton*, *Winnipeg* and *Kikino*. You will be able to find out where those places are by looking at the maps in the book.

You will also learn some new words in this book. While you are reading, you will find some words in **darker print**. You can find out what these words mean by looking at the Glossary in the back of the book.

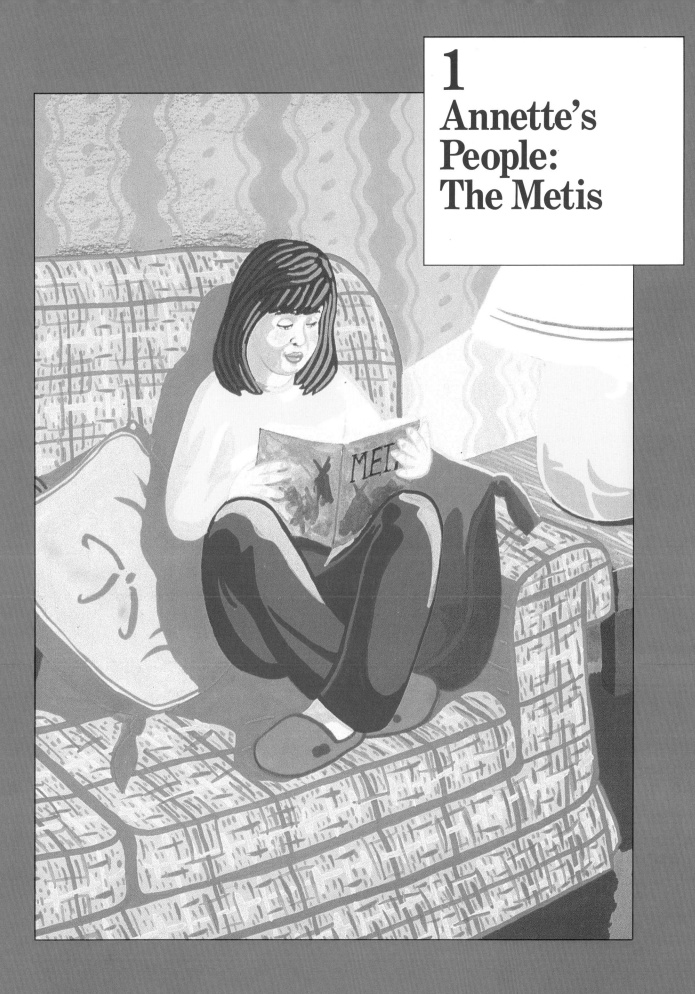

1 Annette Learns about the Metis People

Annette looked out the window. "Dad's home!" she said excitedly. She ran out to meet her Dad. Mr. McKay worked each day as a trainman. He was dressed in his **ViaRail** uniform. He sure looks handsome, Annette thought proudly.

"Hi sweetheart," said Mr. McKay. He picked up Annette. Mr. McKay gave her a big hug. "How was your day?" he asked.

"All right," she answered.

Annette loved to ask questions. Her Dad could tell she was going to ask one now. He wanted to ask her what "all right" meant. But Annette was too quick for him.

"*Dad's home*!"
she said excitedly.

"Dad, have you ever heard of Christopher Columbus?"

"Hmmm." Mr. McKay pretended to think very hard. He gently put Annette down. "Christopher Columbus," he said softly. "Christopher Columbus. Let's see, how did that song go?"

"In fourteen hundred ninety two, Columbus sailed the ocean blue!"

Annette giggled. Mr. McKay was an excellent trainman. He was a good father too. But he was a *terrible* singer!

"Who told you about Christopher Columbus?" he asked his laughing daughter.

"My teacher, Miss Pritchard," Annette answered. "She read us a story about Columbus. He sailed across the Atlantic Ocean and discovered America. Miss Pritchard said Columbus thought he'd come to India. That's why he called the people he met **Indians**. I guess he was a little mixed up!"

"I guess so," chuckled Mr. McKay. "We all make mistakes, even famous **explorers**. Our **ancestors** had lived in America for thousands of years!" he said. "But they never called themselves Indians."

Annette looked confused. "Our ancestors?" she asked. "Are we Indians Dad?"

"Only in part," answered Mr. McKay. "Now, no more questions, Annette. I can't hear them anyway, my stomach is rumbling. I'm starving!"

Annette went upstairs to wash her hands before supper. She kept thinking about what her Dad had said. They were part Indian! Annette decided to wait until the family was at the table. Then she would ask some more questions.

Her brother, Duncan, was in the living room. Duncan was telling his Dad about a basketball game.

Duncan was tall, blond and sixteen. Annette loved him very much. She ran across the room and tried to tackle her big brother. Duncan pretended Annette was too tough for him. He groaned and fell on the rug.

Dinner at the McKay home was a family affair. The table was always properly set. Everyone sat down to eat together. This was Annette's favourite time of the day. It was the *perfect* time to ask questions.

"Mom, will you please pass the milk and are you part Indian too and...."

"Whoa, young lady," replied a laughing Mrs. McKay. "First things first. Here's the milk. And yes, I am part Indian. My **great-grandmother** was a **Cree Indian**."

"And your **great-grandfather**?" Annette asked.

"Mom, will you please pass the milk," said Annette.

5

"My great-grandfather was French-Canadian. He was a **fur trader**," answered Mrs. McKay. "And he was the manager of a **trading post** in northern *Saskatchewan*," she added.

"It's really a very lovely story, Annette," said Mrs. McKay. Great-grandfather lived among the Cree people. He learned to speak their language. He learned to appreciate their way of life. In fact, he fell in love with a young Cree woman. They were married. Many of the families in the area were a mixture of French-Canadian men and Cree Indian women."

"Wow! My ancestors were Cree Indians!" cried Annette.

"Could be, Annette," said Mr. McKay. "And maybe that is where you **inherited** your dark hair and brown eyes . Please pass the salt."

"And where did Annette inherit all of her questions from?" teased Duncan.

"The real question," said Mrs. McKay, "is whose turn is it to do the dishes."

Mr. McKay looked at Annette and grinned. She grinned back. "Don't worry, Dad" she said, "I'll help you tonight."

"The real question," said Mrs. McKay, *"is whose turn is it to do the dishes."*

Mr. McKay told Annette about his ancestors while they did the dishes. His great-grandfather had been a **Northwest Mounted Policeman**. "Great-grandfather helped to keep the peace," said Mr. McKay. "The fur traders, Indians and settlers didn't always get along.

Early Metis families.

"Great-grandfather decided to settle in the west. He married a woman who was **Metis**."

"Metis?" asked Annette, "What does that mean?"

"It is a French-Canadian word," answered Mr. McKay. "Metis means mixed blood. Metis describes people like us. We have Indian and European ancestors. Our blood is a mixture of Indian and European."

"Oh," said Annette. "Where do Metis people live today?" she asked.

"Some Metis, like us, have chosen to live in the city. Some Metis people in the north hunt and trap animals for a living," answered Mr. McKay. Other Metis live on farms in the country. Metis people live in many different communities today."

"How can I learn more about the Metis, Dad?" asked Annette.

7

"Dishes done? Homework done?" asked Mr. McKay. Annette nodded her head. "I have a book about the Metis people. Why don't you sit down and read it after we finish here?"

Annette dried her hands and took the book. She settled comfortably on the living room couch. She did not stop reading until Mrs. McKay said "Bedtime young lady."

"It's so exciting, Mom," said Annette. "I'm afraid I might not be able to sleep!"

"Try anyway!" called Mr. McKay from his favourite chair.

Annette slowly climbed the stairs to her bedroom. There was so much to think about!

She did not stop reading until Mrs. McKay said, "*Bedtime young lady.*"

2 Annette has a Dream

Annette dreamed she was standing on a hill with an Indian woman. The stars were bright above them. A warm wind blew over the hill. The tall grasses bent under the wind and looked like moving waves. A flickering fire cast shadows as tall as the trees below.

"Little sister, I have something to tell you," said the woman.

Annette noticed that the woman's clothes were made of leather. She thought they were beautiful.

"Look into the fire," she said. She threw some twigs onto the flames. Annette saw an Indian camp. **Tipis** were set up everywhere. Some boys were racing their horses. Children were playing tag. Women were working near campfires. The Indians were living in the wilderness. "Who are those people?" Annette asked.

"These people are your ancestors," the woman said. "They lived in harmony with nature. Do not be afraid to search out your past. *Do not be afraid to search out your past. Do not be afraid to search ....*"

"Look into the fire,"
she said.

9

Warm autumn sunshine woke Annette. She rolled over in bed. Annette did not want to wake up. She remembered this was Saturday. No school. And her Dad didn't have to work today. Saturdays were special. Annette jumped out of bed and hurried down the stairs.

In the kitchen, Annette's parents were having coffee. "Good morning sleepy-head," her Dad said. "Did you have sweet dreams?"

Annette smiled. "I guess so," she said. She decided to keep her dream a secret for awhile.

"Dad and I thought that we could take you to the **museum** today, Annette" said Mrs. McKay. "Duncan has a basketball practice today but you'll see some interesting things about Metis people. I think you're going to enjoy it."

"Great!" said Annette.

After breakfast, Annette was ready in record time. She went outside. Duncan was shooting baskets on the driveway. His team, the Crescent Heights Vikings, had a big game coming up.

Duncan was shooting baskets on the driveway.

The McKays arrived at the museum at 10:30 A.M. There were very few people there. The **curator** had time to give them a tour. He showed them a display on the **history** of the Metis people around *Medicine Hat*. There were so many things to look at, Annette didn't know where to begin. "Who's that?" she asked. She pointed to a photograph of a proud looking Northwest Mounted Policeman.

"That's Sergeant J.H.G. Bray," said the curator.

"Who's that?" she asked.

"He was married to Jemima McKay," added Mr. McKay. "She was my great aunt."

"Wow!" said Annette. "Our family is in the museum. Wait till I tell Duncan about this."

Her Mom and Dad laughed. While Mr. and Mrs. McKay looked at another display, the curator told Annette a story about a man named William Hatfield Bliss. "Over 100 years ago, 500 **Sioux** Indians came to Canada. Sioux warriors had just won a famous fight in the United States. They killed many American soldiers at the Battle of the Little Big Horn. William Hatfield Bliss and three other Mounted Policemen met the Sioux when they came to Canada. This was a very important mission," the curator explained.

"The Metis hunted buffalo, like the Indians did. They also farmed, like the Europeans did."

The curator added that there were still members of the Bliss family living in Medicine Hat.

"Come over and look at this, Annette," Mrs. McKay called. "Here is a display examining how some of the Metis lived long ago." Annette learned from the display that for part of the year, they hunted buffalo. For part of the year they farmed small farms.

"It's sort of like they lived two lives," Annette said. "The Metis hunted buffalo, like the Indians did. They also farmed, like the Europeans did. They had the best of both worlds didn't they?"

"That's very true," said the curator. "The Metis in these parts were very **adaptable**."

After an hour of looking at all the displays, the McKays thanked the museum curator and drove home.

"I can't wait to tell my friends everything I've learned about our past," said Annette.

3 Sharing the Family's Past with Friends

On Sunday, the McKays attended the morning **mass** at St. Patrick's Church. Annette loved the beautiful old church.

The **priest** gave a sermon about work. Annette listened carefully because he spoke of farming. She had learned that some Metis were farmers. It was good to work with the land.

"You know, Annette, the McKays have been going to St. Patrick's for years. Your father was baptized there and so were you and Duncan," said Mrs. McKay on the way home.

On Sunday, the McKays attended the morning mass at St. Patrick's Church.

"And it's interesting to think that the church comes from our European ancestors," said Mr. McKay. He looked at Annette in the rear view mirror. She smiled at him. "We have learned from our Indian ancestors to respect nature," he added.

"Hmm," said Annette. "Sometimes I'd like to be an Indian. Other times, I'd like to be a European. Mostly I think I want a little of what both have."

"You've made a good choice," said Mrs. McKay. "You can learn a lot from your ancestors. Be grateful for the good things you have received from both backgrounds."

After lunch, Annette phoned her two best friends Lucy and Fran. She asked them to come over to her house. Annette hung up the receiver and bounced out the door. She sat on the doorstep to wait for her friends.

Soon the three girls were in a little huddle in the McKay's backyard. Annette was talking excitedly. "I am part Indian and part European," said Annette.

"You're what?" asked Lucy. She had a puzzled look on her face.

"You see, Lucy, my Mom is part French and part Cree Indian. My Dad is part Scottish and part Cree Indian. That means that I am part Indian, too," replied Annette. " I'm called a Metis."

"You don't look like an Indian to me," chimed in Fran. "Don't Indians live in tipis and ride pinto ponies and chase buffalo?"

"Don't be silly, Fran," said Annette. "That's story book stuff from the past. Indians drive cars and have jobs in the city, just like anyone else!"

"I am part Indian and part European," said Annette.

"My great-great-grandfather was one of the first Mounted Policemen in the West. He married my great-great grandmother who was part Cree Indian."

"That's the second time you've said Cree. What does that mean?" asked Fran.

"Cree Indians are a group of Indians. They have their own language," answered Annette.

"That's fantastic!" said Lucy. "I don't know where my parents and grandparents came from, but I wish I did. Maybe I am part Indian, too."

"Maybe you are, Lucy. Maybe we even have the same ancestors," agreed Annette. Then she told her friends about her visit to the museum and about the things she had seen there. She was going to tell them about her dream. Then she realized that her friends would probably not understand it. Besides, it was fun to have a secret.

"I'm not part Indian," said Fran, sounding a bit sad. "My parents came from Germany. They don't have any Indians there. But your past seems so — *so romantic*," she said with a sigh.

Metis Historical Dress

Fran had an idea. "Why don't we pretend to live like the people did in the old days? My Mom has some old clothes we could use to dress up in," she suggested.

"Let's", said Annette, "I'll ask my Mom for some clothes too. Maybe I could dress up like the Metis used to."

15

"Why don't we pretend to live like the people did in the old days?"

Annette put on a flowered blouse with full sleeves. She put a black **shawl** around her shoulders. One of Mrs. McKay's old skirts was just the perfect length. It went almost to the ground. Annette used a woven belt to hold the skirt up.

Lucy hurried home and got some old high heeled shoes. She also got two old wigs and a few lady's hats. Fran brought a shawl, a coat and a dress.

For the next hour the girls had fun dressing up and acting like adults.

Then Annette's Mom called from the house, "It's supper time, girls." Mrs. McKay had already phoned Lucy's and Fran's mothers. The girls had permission to stay for supper.

After Lucy and Fran went home that night, Annette went up to her room and got ready for bed.

Somehow the Indian part of her background seemed so unreal. It was just like a fairy-tale. *Just like Fran said*, she thought, *it is romantic*. Annette was glad that her friends were almost as excited about her being Metis as she was. She knew that they would talk about this for a long time.

16

4 A Northern Visit

The next evening, Annette was doing homework at the kitchen table. She was colouring in a map of her own province, Alberta. Part of the assignment was to put her own city on the map. She looked at an atlas and found Medicine Hat.

"Mom and Dad?" Annette asked as she walked into the living room. "Look at this."

Mr. and Mrs. McKay looked at the map. "I see you've put Medicine Hat on the map," said Mrs. McKay.

"Yes," said Annette. "Now I have to colour it."

"My Uncle Mac lives near *Lac La Biche*. Do you know where that is?" asked Mr. McKay.

"No. I don't," said Annette. "Uncle Mac?" she asked. "Is he a Metis?"

"Yes, he is," answered Mr. McKay. "He and his family live in a community where there are quite a few Metis. Lac La Biche is right here." He pointed to a spot in northern Alberta. "*Kikino* is the name of Uncle Mac's community. It is very close to Lac La Biche."

"Are Kikino or Lac La Biche like Medicine Hat?" Annette asked.

Mr. MacKay explained that Lac La Biche was a small town. "Many of the Metis people there live outside the town. Uncle Mac, for example, lives in the wooded area near Lac La Biche.

He traps animals for a living," Mr. McKay said.

Annette's map of Alberta.

"I would love to live in the wooded area of Alberta and go along with you when you hunted and trapped, Dad!" Annette's eyes shone with excitement. This sounded just like her dream. "Do they live in tipis there?" she asked.

"Not so fast, Annette," said Mr. McKay. "The days of living close to nature for most of us are in the past. We Metis want to make our mark in the modern Canada along with all other Canadians. Living in the woods may seem very romantic to you. But there are many exciting things we can do in our own city. I like my job with ViaRail. I am sure you will enjoy your **career** when you grow up. I know you like going to school with all of your friends in Medicine Hat."

Annette took her Dad by the hand. "When can we go up to see Kikino?" she asked.

Mrs. McKay had been listening to the conversation. "You're planning to take some holidays next week, aren't you, Fred?" she asked.

"Yes, from Thursday morning to Monday night," Mr. McKay answered.

Mrs. McKay winked at Annette. "We could leave on Wednesday night, travel to Red Deer and stay overnight in a motel. On Thursday we would be able to drive the rest of the way and arrive early," she said.

"How long would it take to get there?" Annette asked.

"Let's see," said Mr. McKay, studying the map of Alberta. "It is just over 700 kilometres from Medicine Hat to Kikino."

"That would take about seven hours driving," Annette guessed.

"Seven hours!" her Dad exclaimed. "It would take closer to ten hours."

"But Dad, what if you drove 100 kilometres per hour? Kikino is 700 kilometres away. If you divide 100 into 700 you get 7," Annette happily explained.

"Your math is correct, Annette," said Mr. McKay, "But we have to take time to eat and fill the car with gas. Through the towns and cities we can only drive 50 kilometres per hour. All that takes time. We would need ten hours," he said.

"Oh please, Dad! Can we go?" Annette begged. "I would love to see how the people live there."

"Well, I don't know," Mr. McKay said with a frown. "If we go to Kikino you'll have to miss school. You will have to work twice as hard to make up the lost time."

"I will, I promise I will," Annette pleaded. "Please can we go?"

Mr. McKay laughed. "I think we *are* going!" He picked Annette up and gave her a quick hug.

"*Your math is correct, Annette,*" said Mr. Mckay.

5 On the Road

Mr. McKay backed the car down the driveway. They were going to Kikino! Duncan stood at the door and waved goodbye. Annette was sad that Duncan could not come. He had a basketball game on the weekend.

Annette rolled down her window. "Hope you win another game, Duncan!" she called out.

As the McKays drove towards *Calgary*, they talked about the things they saw along the way. They saw **donkey pumps** in the fields along the highway. The pumps bobbed up and down and up and down as they pumped oil. There were crop lands after *Bassano*. Mrs. McKay told them that this was a great wheat farming district. "With all of these fields," said Mr. McKay, "there will probably never be a shortage of wheat."

The road sign showed that the next town would be *Gleichen*. Mr. McKay pointed to the south of the highway and said, "Do you see those distant rolling plains? That's the *Blackfoot Indian Reserve*."

"What's a **reserve**?" Annette wanted to know.

"A reserve," said Mr. McKay. "is land set aside for Indian people to live on."

"Oh," said Annette. "And who are the Blackfoot Indians?"

"The Blackfoot are a group of Indians who have lived on the prairies for hundreds of years," answered Mr. McKay.

As they approached Calgary, the skyscrapers stood out against a blue sky. The McKays stopped at a service station there to fill the gas tank. Then they drove to a small restaurant for supper. Soon they were on their way again. "Many people who live in Calgary work in the oil industry," Mrs. McKay said.

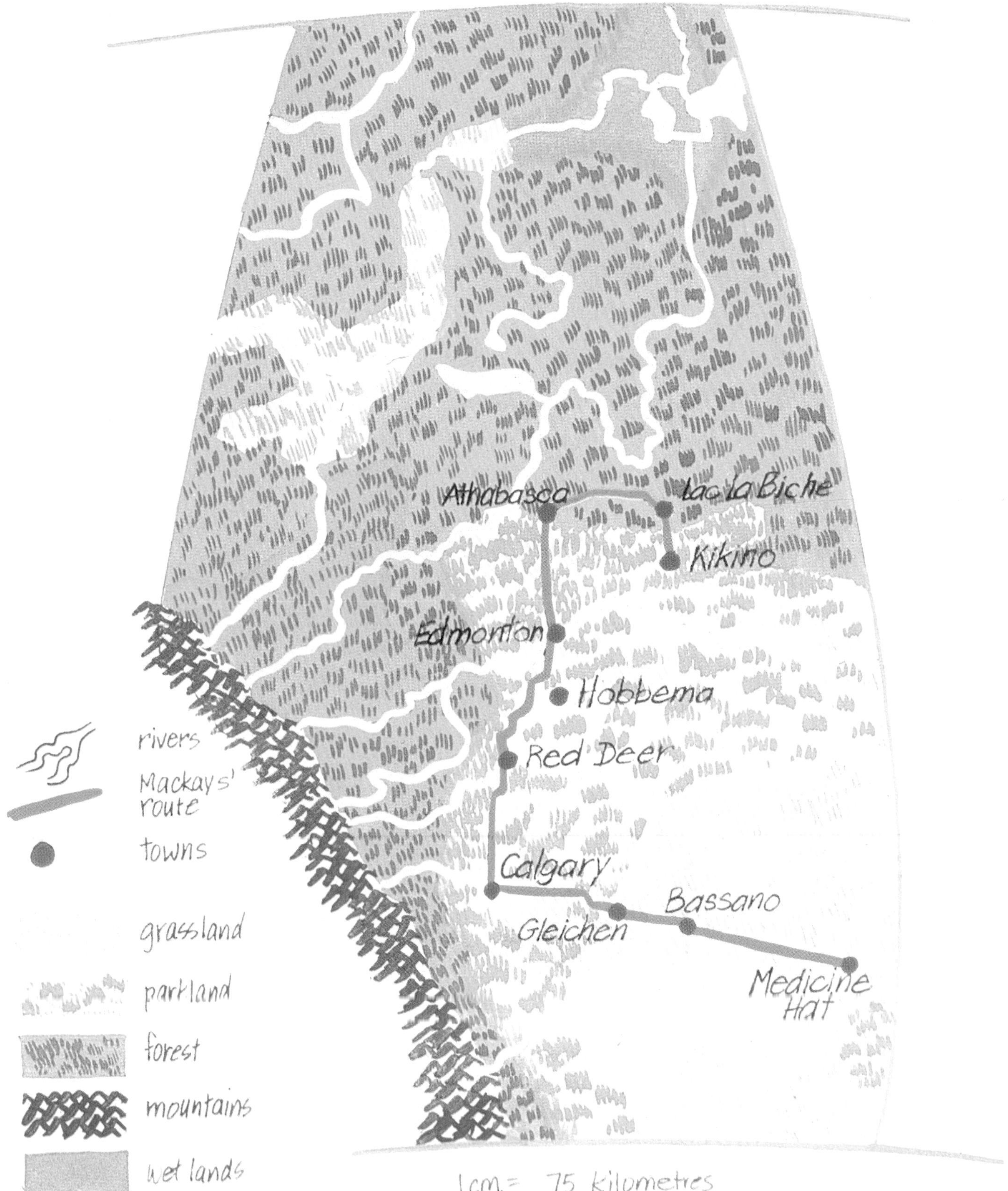

Athabasca
Lac la Biche
Kikino
Edmonton
Hobbema
Red Deer
Calgary
Bassano
Gleichen
Medicine Hat

rivers

Mackays'
route

towns

grassland

parkland

forest

mountains

wet lands

Scale of kilometres

1 cm. = 75 kilometres

"Many Calgarians go skiing and hiking in the mountains," said Mrs. McKay.

Annette could see the Rocky Mountains from the Calgary highway. The mountains were west of the city. "Many Calgarians go skiing and hiking in the mountains," said Mrs. McKay.

When the McKays reached **Red Deer**, they stopped at a motel along the highway. After they had taken their luggage into the motel, Annette persuaded her parents to go for a walk. They noted that there were more small trees or brush here than there was in Medicine Hat.

Annette persuaded her parents to go for a walk.

23

These bands had signed an agreement with the Government of Canada a longtime ago.

Chief Samson

Early next morning Mr. McKay had the luggage back into the car and was waiting while Mrs. McKay and Annette looked around the motel to make sure nothing had been left behind. They were soon heading towards *Edmonton*.

The countryside along the highway was new to Annette. She noticed the big dairy farms. The rolling hills were wooded. They passed a sign that read, *Hobbema*. Mr. McKay explained that around the town of Hobbema there were four Cree Indian **bands**. These bands had signed an agreement with the Government of Canada a long time ago. This agreement is called Treaty No.6.

"Why do the Blackfoot Indians live near Gleichen and the Cree Indians live around Hobbema?" asked Annette.

"That is a long story Annette," said Mr. McKay. "The main reason is that this is the land their ancestors agreed to live on."

The city of Edmonton seemed very big to Annette. When they drove over the *North Saskatchewan River*, Mrs. McKay pointed out the **Legislature** Building. Annette thought that the river valley was very beautiful. Annette learned that many of the people in Edmonton worked for the government.

"We have another 275 kilometres to go, so let's keep moving," Mrs. McKay encouraged.

Mrs. McKay pointed out the Legislature Building.

North of Edmonton, tall spruce trees lined the sides of the highway. Often they could only see straight ahead. At **Athabasca** they turned east along Highway No. 55 until they reached Lac La Biche. Then they turned south and soon Annette read the sign, Kikino. She was getting quite excited about meeting her relatives. Her Mom had told her a little about what she might expect.

"Remember, these people are not living in the city where all roads are paved and water is brought to the houses in pipes. Their houses are separated some distance from each other," Mrs. McKay explained. "The roads are often rough. At night there are no street lights."

They turned into the lane leading to Uncle Mac's and Aunt Joyce's home. The late afternoon sun was shimmering through the trees. Yellow and red leaves were thick on the laneway and on their lawn. The white **bungalow** looked cosy.

The front door of the cabin opened and Uncle Mac waved hello. He was very tall. He had long gray hair. He was wearing blue jeans and **moccasins**.

Aunt Joyce was also tall. She had a friendly smile. Her long dark hair was loose about her shoulders. Annette thought she looked pretty.

"Welcome, welcome!" said Uncle Mac. "Did you have a good trip?" He slapped Mr. McKay on the back and shook his hand. Then he came around to the other side and helped Mrs. McKay out of the car. Annette got out and smiled at him.

"Hello, Uncle Mac. Hello, Aunt Joyce" she said.

"Well hello there!" he replied. "Welcome to Kikino. You must be Annette."

"Welcome, welcome!" said Uncle Mac. "Did you have a good trip?"

26

6 Cousin Joey

"Hello, Joey," greeted Annette, *"I'm pleased to meet you."*

Inside, Annette saw a boy at the kitchen table. Aunt Joyce introduced them.

"Annette, this is your cousin Joey. Joey stays with us while he is going to school."

"Hello, Joey," greeted Annette, "I'm pleased to meet you."

"Hello, Annette," replied Joey, "I'm please to meet you, too. Aunt Joyce told me you were coming and asked me to show you around Kikino tomorrow."

The talk in the house was lively for the next hour. Annette learned that Joey was two years older than she was. He was eleven.

Soon Aunt Joyce called them to have supper. Uncle Mac had been moose hunting. For supper they had roast moose meat with their vegetables. Annette thought that the meat looked a bit dark but it was delicious!

After supper Joey said "I want you to tell me everything about yourself in the morning. I have lots of questions like: Where's Medicine Hat? How long did it take to get here? Do you have any brothers or sisters? But its late and I'd better let you get some sleep first." Joey had been to a city only a few times and he was very curious.

Aunt Joyce showed Annette to the room she would share with her parents. There were some blankets on a small cot in the corner where Annette would sleep.

Annette was up early the next morning. It was going to be a nice day. Pretty soon everyone was up. Well, almost everyone. Joey came out of his room looking sleepy. Once he saw that pancakes were for breakfast, he woke up!

At breakfast, Uncle Mac explained what they would do that day. "Joey, once you are finished eating every pancake in sight, I would like you to help me catch the horses. Give them a good brush down and then we will hitch them to the wagon. We are going on a special, old-fashioned outing today. We'll leave the cars and trucks in the garage, and ride in style!"

Joey grinned, "Okay, Uncle Mac! Can Annette help me with the horses?"

"I don't know, Joey," said Uncle Mac. "You had better ask her yourself." Annette quickly agreed to help Joey.

Uncle Mac explained that they could drive around the settlement and see some of the neighbours. Then they could drive to the *Amisk River* in the afternoon and do a little fishing.

Uncle Mac had a team of two large horses. Annette was surprised at how big the horses were. They seemed very gentle, though. Joey taught her how to brush the horses. She watched Joey put their harnesses on. He hitched them to the wagon. The wagon had rubber tires and a box on it. Across the front he had

Joey grinned, *"Okay, Uncle Mac! Can Annette help me with the horses?"*

put a board for the adults to sit on. At the back of the box he had piled some clean straw where Annette and Joey could sit by themselves.

As they drove along Joey told Annette about life at Kikino. "I like it here," he said. "School is okay, but it is the other things that I like best. Sometimes Uncle Mac takes me along when he goes moose hunting," Joey continued.

"How do you hunt moose, Joey?" Annette wanted to know.

"Well, at this time of the year, the bulls fight each other for the cows. Uncle Mac goes into the woods and imitates the call of the bull moose. Soon a bull comes crashing through the bush looking for a fight. When he comes close enough, Uncle Mac can shoot him. My job is to help him skin the moose and cut up the meat."

"What do you do with all that meat?" asked Annette.

"We cut it into strips and hang it on poles. Then we build a smoking fire under it. That's the way meat is dried and smoked.

"What do you do with all that meat?" asked Annette.

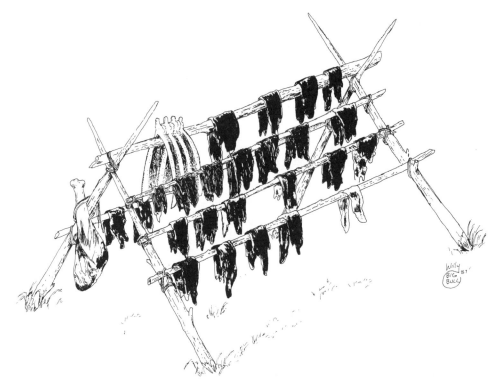

Then it does not spoil. Aunt Joyce cuts some meat into roast size and wraps it for freezing. I like fresh roasted moose meat the best.

"Sometimes I like to go into the woods with Uncle Mac," said Joey. "I like the quiet of the bush. In a few weeks we will set out a **trap line**. When we go out to check if we have caught any animals in the traps, we take smoked moose meat to eat along the way. But, look! We are almost at the Amisk River! Hooray! Now we can go fishing!"

"During mating season, the bulls can be dangerous." said Uncle Mac.

30

Aunt Joyce picked out a cozy spot surrounded by trees, but where there was sunshine. Then she brought out several cans of juice and sandwiches. The sandwiches were made of **bannock** and had smoked meat inside.

As they were eating, Uncle Mac suddenly raised his hand and whispered "sh sh." Everyone froze. Suddenly, **upwind**, a cow moose walked into the open towards the river. Shortly after, a crashing sound and a high pitched call came from the bush where the cow had come out. Then a big antlered bull moose stepped out. As he looked around, he saw the picnickers and made a few threatening steps in their direction. Uncle Mac just motioned for them to be still. Soon the cow caught the bull's attention and he trotted off towards the river.

"During mating season, the bulls can be dangerous," said Uncle Mac.

After lunch they began to fish in the river. Annette had never fished before and Joey was kept busy helping her cast her hook. He helped her to untangle her fishing line when she cast it into the trees instead of into the river. Then, all at once, she felt a sharp tug on the hook.

"We'll have it for supper," said Aunt Joyce.

"Joey! I've got one!" she shouted. "Come and help me bring him in." She began to crank on the reel. Little by little she brought the fish to the shore. Joey reminded her to keep the line tight. The fish finally flopped on the shore. Joey took the hook out of the fish's mouth and held it up for everyone to see. It was a **Northern Pike**. The fish was a good size. Annette danced about with excitement as her fish was being admired.

"We'll have it for supper," said Aunt Joyce.

As the sun was setting they drove back to the cabin. On the way, Joey told Annette more about Uncle Mac's trap line. "Uncle Mac traps squirrel, mink, and beaver. That is how he makes his living," Joey explained. "He sells the furs at the local **fur auction**. We learned in school that the Metis people have always been an important part of the fur trade in Canada."

The weekend seemed short to Annette. After supper on Sunday, Mr. McKay got up from the table and said that they would have to leave early in the morning for the long journey home.

Joey helped Annette collect some cones and leaves for a collection. Aunt Joyce gave Annette a beautiful pair of soft **mukluks**. She had made them from moose hide and had decorated them with flowery embroidery. Annette decided to wear the mukluks, instead of her shoes, on the way home.

Aunt Joyce gave Annette a beautiful pair of soft mukluks.

Uncle Mac gave them some smoked moose meat to take home.

The next morning the McKays said good-bye to their relatives and set out on their journey. Annette sat in the back seat. For a long time she sat thinking. She did not even ask her parents any questions. Annette had seen how some of the Metis lived in the wooded area of Alberta. *People seem freer here than in the city,* Annette thought.

7 Early Lifestyles and Migrations

Duncan and Annette were setting the supper table. "Did you know that Uncle Bill is coming over tonight?" said Annette.

"I haven't seen Uncle Bill for a long time," said Duncan. "Since you're so interested in history, I guess you will be eager to hear about Uncle Bill's family. The Crockfords are one of the earliest families living in the Medicine Hat area."

"Is Uncle Bill Metis like we are?" asked Annette.

"You'll have to ask Uncle Bill that yourself. Does it matter?" replied Duncan.

"Of course it matters," Annette answered. "It is always important to know who you are. Miss Pritchard calls it our **identity**. She told us that we could understand ourselves better if we knew where we came from."

Mr. McKay and Mr. Crockford arrived at the same time. Annette could hear them talking as they came to the door. She ran out to meet them. "Hello, Daddy! Hello, Uncle Bill," she called.

"Well hello, Annette," answered Mr. Crockford. "It's been so long since I've seen you. Good gracious, how you've grown."

"Hello, Daddy! Hello, Uncle Bill," she called.

91- 1400

BANFF TRAIL EL

35

"Uncle Bill," asked Annette, "do you know much about the Metis?"

"Easy does it," said Mr. McKay. "Let's wait until we're at the table before all the questions start."

Annette nodded her head. "Okay, Daddy," she said. She was shy for a moment.

Mrs. McKay called everyone to the table.

"Rachel, your cooking is always so good!" said Mr. Crockford to Mrs. McKay. They went into the dining room. Mr. Crockford pulled out a chair for Annette to sit on. "To answer your question, Annette, I am Metis. And I know a lot about the Metis in this part of the province." Mr. Crockford took his place at the table. He sat across from Annette. He passed Duncan the bread.

"The early Metis would often eat bannock," explained Mr. Crockford. "They made all of their own food. They did not buy it at a store. Bannock was their bread.

"The early Metis would often eat bannock," explained Mr. Crockford.

"Another food that they made was **pemmican**. It was made from dried buffalo meat and berries. **Venison**, **elk** and moose were some of the other types of meat they would eat.

"What kinds of desserts did they have back then?" asked Annette.

"My grandmother could bake excellent **saskatoon** pie. Every summer in early August she would take her family, including grandchildren, out to pick berries with her," answered Mr. Crockford.

"My Mom bakes delicious saskatoon pie, too," said Annette. "We go saskatoon picking every summer."

"Then you can understand why the Metis enjoyed saskatoon pie," said Mr. McKay.

During supper they talked about other aspects of Metis life. Annette was very interested. "Could you start from the beginning Uncle Bill," she said. "Where did the Metis people come from? Were they here before the Mounted police came, or did they come with the police?"

"There were Metis people here before the Northwest Mounted Police came," said Mr. Crockford. "I should tell you a little about my great-grandfather, Sergeant Bray," he continued. "Great-grandfather was one of the Northwest Mounted Police. They came from the east and crossed **Lake Superior** by boat. From there they travelled by the Dawson Road to **Fort Garry**. Fort Garry is now called **Winnipeg**.

"From there they continued west, on horseback, to southern Alberta. They had their supplies and equipment loaded on wagons."

"But why did they come? Who sent them? Why didn't the Metis have their own police?" Annette asked.

"You do want to know everything, don't you!?" Mr. Crockford asked.

Annette nodded her head.

Mr. Crockford continued his story. "Life in Alberta was different long ago. Many of the Metis were hunters. They moved here because there were more buffalo. Some of the Metis came to the Cypress Hills area. Others went to the more northerly parts of the province.

"By the 1870s, more than one hundred years ago, the buffalo herds did not come as far north as they once had. The Metis then hunted for them across the U.S. border. This brought them in touch with American traders. Some of the traders didn't care

"Life in Alberta was different long ago. Many of the Metis were hunters."

about being good to the Metis and Indians. Making money was more important to them.

"They brought **whiskey** to trade for furs and pemmican. These whiskey traders brought a sad time for both the Natives and the European settlers. The whiskey made people drunk. Sometimes they got drunk and hurt themselves or each other.

"One day some of these traders, after drinking too much whiskey, came upon an Indian camping site. They killed all of the men, women and children. It was Mr. Edward McKay, your great-great grandfather, who sent word to the Canadian government of this terrible crime. It was known as the Cypress Hills **Massacre**."

"Were the murderers caught and put in jail?" asked Annette angrily.

Mr. Crockford shook his head. "No," he answered. "But the police were sent west to stop the whiskey trade. That's why the Northwest Mounted Police came to Alberta."

And that's when Sergeant Bray came to Alberta!" guessed Annette.

"That's right, Annette," said Mr. Crockford. "Your father should tell you how Sergeant Bray came to meet Jemima McKay."

"Okay, Bill," said Mr. McKay to Mr. Crockford. "I guess I can take up the story from there!" He laughed. "Jemima's father, Edward McKay, was living in the Cypress Hills. He had five daughters. One of the policemen went for an evening ride to enjoy the scenery. He rode over the hills. In one valley he saw a log cabin and some barns. There were several girls working around the place. He rode up to the yard and talked to them. The constable returned to camp. He reported that he had found Paradise, complete with five beautiful girls!

"The next day, Sergeant Bray brought four other Mounted policemen to the McKay home. They were all invited to stay for supper. The Mounties built their fort close to the McKay home.

*"He rode over the hills.
In one valley he saw a
log cabin and some
barns."*

They visited the family often. A year later, Sergeant Bray
married Jemima McKay.''

"And they lived happily ever after!" laughed Annette. "It sounds
like a fairy tale. Is it really true?"

"Indeed it is!" answered Mr. Crockford. "After all, they are my
great-grandparents.''

"And how did they get to Medicine Hat?" asked Annette.

"My great-grandfather retired from the police force in 1882 and
began to ranch in the *Pincher Creek* area," replied Mr.
Crockford. "After ten years he came to Medicine Hat where he
worked for the government as a **stock inspector**. He lived here
until his death in 1923.

"Now it's getting late. I must be going home," he said. He
thanked Mr. and Mrs. McKay for the dinner. "And thank you for
being such good listeners, Annette and Duncan," he said.

"Good-night, Uncle Bill," she said, "thank you for coming over
to talk to us tonight."

8 Camping in the Cypress Hills

The Friday night of the Thanksgiving weekend was a busy time for the McKays. Every autumn Annette's family drove to the Cypress Hills to camp. Mr. McKay checked and loaded the camper trailer. Mrs. McKay prepared food to take along. Duncan rolled up the sleeping bags and cleaned up the camp stove. Annette packed a little suitcase just for herself with some clothes, a toothbrush and a towel. She took her camera along just in case she saw a deer or a moose. The Cypress Hills were very different from the city.

Saturday dawned clear and warm. The McKays were on the road by 8:00 a.m. As they rounded the bend near *Elkwater Lake*, Duncan cried out, "Wow! Look at that! I'm always amazed by Elkwater Lake. On the north side of the lake there's nothing but grass. On the south side there are beautiful trees. Why is that, Dad?" he asked.

"What you're looking at is the dividing line between prairie and the mountains," explained Mr. McKay. "It's possible that the Cypress Hills were never covered by ice during the **Ice Age**. This is why some of the plants and animals we have here cannot be found anywhere else in Alberta. The **altitude** also affects the

As they rounded the bend near Elkwater Lake, Duncan cried out, *"Wow! Look at that!"*

41

kinds of plants that can grow here. Many of the plants are similar to those found in the *Waterton Lakes* area."

In less than an hour, the McKays were at the camp grounds near Elkwater Lake. They set up camp. Mrs. McKay told the family that an **archaeologist** was in the Cypress Hills area. The archaeologist, Gerry Davison, was collecting information about the Metis. Metis people used to live in the Cypress Hills during the winter. Mrs. Davison was looking for clues about how the Metis used to live. Mr. McKay suggested that they go to look for the archaeologist.

They drove towards the southwest end of the Cypress Hills.

"What's that over there?" asked Annette. She pointed out the window.

"Some bushes and a few trucks," said Duncan. "Maybe that's where the archaeologists are digging."

The McKays drove slowly towards the parked trucks. They parked their truck near some mounds of dirt. There were people working nearby.

"Are you the archaeologists who are looking for Metis artifacts?"

Mrs. McKay approached them. "Good morning, I'm Rachel McKay and this is my family," she said. "Are you the archaeologists who are looking for Metis **artifacts**?"

"Good morning to you!" answered one of the workers. "If you're looking for the **Kajewski Cabin** site, you've found it. The person in charge here is Gerry Davison. I'll get her for you."

42

Soon a woman climbed out of one of the places they were digging. "Hi, I'm Gerry Davison. What can I do for you?"

Mrs. McKay introduced Duncan and Mr. McKay. Annette was so excited, she introduced herself.

"I'm Annette and we're Metis," said Annette. "We heard you were here and we wanted to talk to you. Is this really an old Metis camping area?" Annette wanted to know.

"I'm very pleased to meet you, Annette," said Mrs. Davison. "We are fairly sure that this is an old Metis **hivernant** village site. We are looking for clues to support that idea. It won't look like it did when the Metis lived here long ago. Trees and grasses have grown over the village site. Archaeologists have to dig to find evidence that the Metis were here." She explained that the Metis who lived in winter villages were known as *Les Hivernants*. "That's French for winter settlers," she said.

"If Metis people lived here during the winter, where did they live in the summer time?" asked Duncan.

"That's a good question, " said Mrs. Davison. "There was a large community of Metis people living in Manitoba. For a number of reasons, some of the Metis decided to leave. One of the reasons was because their way of life was changing. More **immigrants** moved into Manitoba. These people did not follow the Metis way of life. They didn't like to move about in search of buffalo or other animals. They preferred to live in a city or on nearby farms.

"During the winter, they would settle in one area, like the Cypress Hills. During the summer they could hunt and trap. They were living away from cities and closer to nature. Just before winter began, they moved to places like this. They moved to sheltered **coulees** or treed areas and built log huts."

"Why would they choose this place?" asked Duncan. "I could think of many other, more comfortable places."

"There are several important reasons why this area could be a good winter area," answered Mrs. Davison. "First of all, you will notice the creek nearby. That's where they got their water." She pointed to the south. "Look south towards the ***Sweet Grass Hills***. See all the grazing land? This is where the buffalo and other game animals would feed during the winter. The Cypress Hills area was good for trapping small fur animals. So you see, they planned quite well when they located here."

"How many people would live in one of these settlements?" asked Mr. McKay.

"Sometimes there were as many as 200 people in one village," answered Mrs. Davison.

"What did the kids do during the winter months? Did they have schools? Or did they get their lessons through the mail?" asked Annette.

Mrs. Davison chuckled. "No, Annette, there were no school lessons sent through the mail in those days. Some villages, though, had priests who taught the children how to read and write."

"Oh," said Annette.

44

Mrs. Davison smiled at her. "Most of the children did not learn to read and write. They played with home-made toys like buffalo-hide sleds. The boys became very good at snaring small animals, especially rabbits. The small animals were used for food and their skins for clothing. The older girls often helped prepare animal hides and clothes. They did fancy bead and **embroidery** work on their clothes. Bigger villages had a large cabin where the

"They played with home-made toys like buffalo-hide sleds."

priest held church services and where dances were held. When there was a dance, the children were always included."

"Why did the Metis move away from here? Where did they go?" asked Annette.

"That is kind of sad," explained Mrs. Davison. "The priests knew that the **nomadic lifestyle** of the Metis would end when the buffalo were all killed off. The priests encouraged the Hivernants to settle in one place. They suggested that the Metis farm. But the Metis did not want to do this. The Metis considered themselves free people. They thought it was too boring to live in one place for too long."

"But the buffalo did die off, didn't they?" asked Duncan.

"Yes, Duncan, they did. And the Metis continued to hunt and move about. Now they were hunting other animals. Many of the Metis families moved far to the north where the land is forested. In 1882, the last small, wild herd of buffalo was sighted near present day *Irvine*. Then no more buffalo came to graze on the Canadian prairies.

"Those who hunted and trapped were happy to live in the north. Here few European settlers would interfere with their free way

45

of life. Some, however, began to work for the ranchers and farmers. Others settled in Medicine Hat where they almost forgot their Metis ancestors. People are often forced by circumstances to change their ways."

"Most of the Metis people we know live in the city. I'm not sure I want to go back to living in a log cabin during the winter with no T.V.!" said Annette.

"You're right," replied Mrs. Davison. "The Metis of today are an important part of Canadian society. Many have learned to make themselves comfortable in the cities."

"It has been most kind of you, Mrs. Davison, to spend so much of your time answering our questions. Thank you very much. Good luck on your search for artifacts and clues," said Mrs. McKay. "We'll let you get back to your work. Thanks again!"

As the McKays drove away, Annette waved to Mrs. Davison. She felt that she had learned more about her people. She looked forward to camping out that evening.

"I'm not sure I want to go back to living in a log cabin during the winter with no T.V.!" said Annette.

46

9 The Train Ride to Winnipeg

One day, Mr. McKay came home from work and he looked very happy. He was smiling. He threw his hat up into the air and caught it.

"ViaRail has given me a family pass to *Winnipeg*. Would you like to go to Winnipeg, Annette?" he asked. Mr. McKay put his trainman's hat on Annette's head. It slipped down over her eyes. Everyone laughed.

"Daddy!" said Annette. She pushed the hat back on her head. "All aboard!" she cried. "We are going to Winnipeg!"

Early on Thursday morning, the McKays were waiting on the station platform. Soon the train came around the bend towards the station. When it stopped, the **conductor** helped Annette and Mrs. McKay up the steps into the coach. They found a spot near the middle where there were four free seats. They sat facing each other.

"All aboard!" she cried. *"We are going to Winnipeg!"*

After the conductor had checked their tickets, Mr. McKay suggested that they go into the dining car to have breakfast. While the McKays ordered breakfast, they watched the rolling prairie hills pass by.

After breakfast, Duncan and Annette went up to the **dome car** where the sun roof opened to the sky. They watched as the train sped across the prairie. It was almost noon when it pulled into *Regina*. They ran back down to the coach car where their parents were.

"Tell us about Regina," Annette asked as she settled in beside her mother.

"Regina is one of the early settlements of the west," Mrs. McKay explained. "It became a city in 1882 and for over twenty years was the capital city of the *Northwest Territories*. The Northwest Mounted Police had their headquarters here."

The train rolled along, picking up speed. As the train crossed the beautiful *Qu' Appelle Valley*, Mr. McKay explained that the town of Qu'Appelle had been a Metis settlement until the immigrant farmers began to settle there.

It was late when the train finally pulled into the Winnipeg station. The lights and the noise of the city frightened Annette a little. She stayed close to her parents. When they had picked up their luggage, Mr. McKay called a taxi to take them to their hotel. After a long day of travel, they were soon fast asleep.

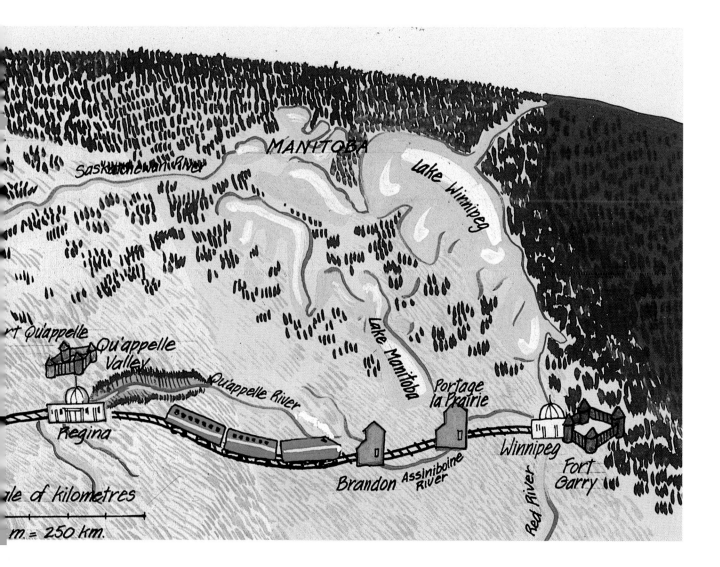

"I move that we go see **Fort Garry** first," said Annette the next morning.

"I second the motion," said Duncan.

"I move we go to the museum first," argued Mr. McKay.

"Mom, please don't make it a tie! Please vote with Duncan and me," begged Annette.

"It is a beautiful day outside, and I would like to see old Fort Garry," said Mrs. McKay. "I vote with the children. Let's go to Fort Garry on the bank of the famous **Red River**," Mrs. McKay replied as she smiled smugly at Mr. McKay.

"You're outvoted, Dad," chuckled Annette. "Let's get going."

"I think I'm being ganged up on," pouted Mr. McKay. He telephoned for a taxi and they drove out to Fort Garry.

The old fort had been completely restored. The walls were built of field stone and concrete. There were **gun ports** in the walls. Several brass cannon mounted on large wooden wheels stood in the yard. There was a large square near the centre of the fort. Indians dressed in traditional costumes danced to the beat of a drum.

"I move that we go see Fort Garry first," said Annette the next morning.

Annette ran from the brass cannons to the gun ports. She looked out over the high fortress walls. Duncan watched the dancers. Annette came up and tapped him on the shoulder. "Look at that weird-looking wagon over there," Annette pointed. The wagon had two huge wheels and a box with some wooden rails around the top. It was being pulled by a large brown ox.

Mr. and Mrs. McKay came over to Annette and Duncan. "That's the famous **Red River cart**," explained Mrs. McKay. "That is what the Metis travelled in during the old days."

"I want a ride in it," said Annette. She ran over to the cart. The man on the cart shouted out, "Hello!" as he saw her running towards the cart.

"So you want a ride, do you little Miss?" the jolly driver said as he jumped down from the driver's seat. He picked Annette up and set her on the wide driver's bench. Then he got on himself. Duncan jumped in the back of the cart. Mr. and Mrs. McKay waved at their children.

"Hey, hey!" he shouted at the ox. "Get up, let's go! Move out!" The wagon creaked as the ox moved slowly along. They drove around the fort for awhile.

"Did you make this cart yourself?" asked Duncan.

"Hey, hey!" he shouted at the ox. *"Get up, let's go! Move out!"*

"What would he use bones for?" asked Annette.

"I sure did," he replied. "My Grandpa was a Metis trader and he used one of these to travel around."

"Are you Metis?" Annette was surprised.

"Of course," he answered.

"We are too," said Annette. "Tell me more about your grandfather and how he lived," she coaxed.

"There were still a few buffalo around when my Grandpa was a young man. But their bones were scattered all over the plains. Grandpa went around with his cart and gathered the bones. He took the bones to the nearest railway station. The **agent** at the railway gave him money for the bones."

"What would he use bones for?" asked Annette.

"The bones were sent to the East where they were used as **fertilizer**. Grandpa did not make much money, but he made a living for his family. In the winter he would cut up trees for firewood and haul it to the settlers in his Red River cart. Sometimes the settlers would hire him to haul grain or other things to and from the railway," explained the driver.

When the ride was over Mr. McKay paid the driver and thanked him for giving Annette and Duncan a ride. "During the last century those carts were very important to the Metis," he said to Annette. "The Red River carts were often the only way of moving needed goods to areas where there were no railways."

The next day the family toured the Winnipeg museum. Annette saw a large **panorama** of the buffalo on the great plains. She tried to imagine living in those bygone days when the buffalo roamed the prairies. The big **beasts** must have been dangerous, she thought.

"A long time ago, there would have been great herds of buffalo grazing on the prairie," said Mrs. McKay.

"That would have been quite a sight," said Mr. McKay. "Do you know that the herds were so large that you would have been able to see buffalo as far as the **horizon**!"

"Really?" asked Duncan, "What happened to them?"

"The buffalo hides made excellent coats. Buffalo tongue was very good to eat. The Metis and others made a living by killing buffalo and selling the hides and meat," said Mrs. McKay. "After years of shooting the buffalo with rifles, the buffalo were almost **extinct**."

Are they all gone now?" asked Annette.

"No, there are large herds at ***Wood Buffalo National Park*** in northern Alberta, and at ***Elk Island National Park***, near Edmonton," Mrs. McKay answered.

"A long time ago, there would have been great herds of buffalo grazing on the prairie," said Mrs. McKay.

They also saw a large **schooner**. Annette's mom reminded her that this was the kind of ship in which her European ancestors came to Canada.

Early the next morning the McKays boarded their train to return home. Annette was sorry to leave Winnipeg but she was anxious to get back to Medicine Hat. She couldn't wait to tell Lucy and Fran about the many new things she had seen. Perhaps she would even write a report in school and give it the title *My Winnipeg Adventure*!

She couldn't wait to tell Lucy and Fran about the many new things she had seen.

10 Hard Times - The Great Depression

"What's **unemployment**?" Lucy asked Miss Pritchard on Monday morning. "I hear the word on television and Dad talks about it sometimes."

"When people are **employed** they have a job," Miss Pritchard explained. "If a person loses their job, then they are unemployed.

"If that happened now, then the government would help until they could find a job again. While they are working they pay money to the **Unemployment Insurance Commission**. If they lose their job they are paid some money by the Commission while they look for more work. There have been times in Canada's history when many people found it hard to make a living because there were very few jobs. One of these times was The Great Depression."

"The Great Depression!" exclaimed Annette. "What was that?"

"The Great Depression!" exclaimed Annette. *"What was that?"*

Miss Pritchard told the class what had happened. "The Great Depression began in 1929. Many businesses and **industries** had to close because they could not sell their **goods**. On the prairies there were also several years of bad weather. Farmers found it hard to grow crops. Dry winds whipped up the topsoil into big dust storms. These years are still called '**The Dirty Thirties**' by older people who lived through them. All this caused much **hardship**. To find work, men and women had to travel to the cities. But there was very little work for people in the cities. To keep people from starving, the government and churches set up **soup kitchens**. Two times a day hungry people would line up for a bowl of soup and a piece of bread."

"Whatever would cause such a bad thing to happen?" one of the students asked Miss Pritchard.

"There were many reasons," their teacher replied. "Because other countries were also poor they could not afford to buy Canadian goods. Many workers lost their jobs because industries could not sell the things they were making. Many people had

"Dry winds whipped up the topsoil into big dust storms."

56

been buying goods on credit. When they lost their jobs they could not pay for the things they needed. Farmers could not sell their grain. You will remember that most of the people in western Canada lived on farms at that time. There were many other reasons, but we won't discuss them now."

After school Annette and her friends walked home together. They were still discussing The Great Depression.

"I wonder if a great depression could happen again," said Lucy.

"I sure hope not," replied Annette.

The following Saturday a visitor came to the McKay's home. Mrs. Julia Bliss Newhart was an older lady who had grown up in the Medicine Hat district. She was the youngest daughter of William Hatfield Bliss, who had come to Medicine Hat as a member of the Northwest Mounted Police. Aunt Julia knew a great deal about the history of southern Alberta.

"Many of them moved
to northern Alberta to
hunt and trap for a
living."

"We talked about The Great Depression in school this week," Annette told Aunt Julia. What happened to the Metis in Medicine Hat at that time?"

"The Metis had not settled down in any one place," Aunt Julia began. "Because they loved their freedom they moved around the country working for farmers and ranchers. When the dry years of the Dirty Thirties came many of them moved to northern Alberta to hunt and trap for a living. This way they could live off the land. Those who stayed in Medicine Hat continued to live by doing odd jobs. Some of the families built small houses on pieces of land that no one else was using. Some people called them **squatters**. Today, the one area where they lived is called *Saratoga Park*."

"I've heard of Saratoga Park, but I've never been there," said Annette. "Could we go and see it, Dad?"

"If Aunt Julia will go with us, we could drive over there right now," her father replied.

"I'd love to go for a little ride," Aunt Julia said.

Soon they were heading over to Saratoga Park. It was near the

"I've heard of Saratoga Park, but I've never been there," said Annette.

old Ogilvie **flour mill**. They parked the car near Seven Persons Creek. Aunt Julia led the way across a foot bridge to the area where several Metis families used to live. Much of the area was now vegetable gardens, but there were still a few old buildings.

"This is where several families used to live until quite recently," explained Aunt Julia. Some of them have died and others have moved away. I still remember the fine times we used to have here. We didn't have any money, but we had good times and good friends."

Aunt Julia explained that some of the Metis girls had done housework for the richer people for twenty five cents a day. Sometimes these girls didn't get paid any **wages**. All they got was some food and used clothes.

"I know of one man who worked on a farm all year just for **room and board**," she said.

"How did The Great Depression end?" asked Annette.

"It took a war to end it," Aunt Julia answered. "**World War II** began in Europe and many of our young men joined the army. Soon the people in Europe needed more food and our farmers were able to sell their grain. Industries began to build guns and tanks and airplanes. Workers who were unemployed went back to work in factories. That's how it ended. The war was hard on our people but the country began to **prosper**."

11 Remembrance Day

November 11 was **Remembrance Day** and there was a school holiday. Daisy Bliss Legere, a Metis friend of the McKay family had promised to take Annette to the **Memorial Services** held at Memorial Park near the South Saskatchewan River.

"I'm ready!" Annette called when Aunt Daisy arrived. "Where are we going to watch the parade?"

"I think it would be best to stand in front of City Hall. Then we can watch the marchers arrive at the park where they hold the service." said Aunt Daisy.

Soon they were watching the men and women of the **Canadian Legion** march by. All the marchers wore bright red **poppies** on their chests. Many of them had medals pinned to their jackets as well. Aunt Daisy explained that they had earned their medals as soldiers in World War II.

"I'm ready!" Annette called when Aunt Daisy arrived. *"Where are we going to watch the parade?"*

Soon they were watching the men and women of the Canadian Legion march by.

"World War II!", exclaimed Annette. "Aunt Julia mentioned that last Saturday. How did the war start?"

"The war began in September of 1939 when **Nazi** Germany **invaded** Poland." Aunt Daisy began. "Britain and the other Commonwealth countries decided to fight against the Hitler **dictatorship**. Canada sent over half a million soldiers overseas to help win the war. Many soldiers died or were wounded. Those are the ones we are remembering today."

When all the parade had gone to Memorial Park, the people who had been watching followed them to the **cenotaph**.

"Whose statue is that, Aunt Daisy?" Annette asked in a whisper.

"It's like putting flowers on the grave of some we knew and loved," Aunt Daisy whispered back. *"The wreaths show that we remember those who died in the war."*

"Whose statue is that, Aunt Daisy?" Annette asked in a whisper.

"It's a statue of an unknown soldier. It reminds us of all the soldiers who died in the wars," explained Aunt Daisy.

The band began to play 'O Canada' and everyone stood at attention. Many sang the words. A minister said a prayer. Then people began placing wreaths at the foot of the cenotaph.

"Why are they doing that?" Annette whispered.

"It's like putting flowers on the grave of someone we knew and loved," Aunt Daisy whispered back. "The wreaths show that we remember those who died in the war."

After the bugle player had played '**The Last Post**,' people began to leave the park. Annette and Aunt Daisy got into the car and headed for home.

"Did you know any soldiers from here who went to war?" asked Annette.

"Yes, Dear," answered Aunt Daisy. "I had four uncles who were in **World War I**. All of them received medals for bravery."

"Did you know any soldiers from here who went to war?" asked Annette.

"Bravery! What do you mean?" asked Annette.

"When a soldier did something that was very dangerous to save the lives of his fellow soldiers, he was often given a medal for being so brave," Aunt Daisy explained.

"My Uncle William was married while he was overseas. His wife and children were killed in an air raid in England," she continued.

"I don't like wars," Annette said. "Why do people want to shoot each other, anyway?"

"That, my Dear, is a hard question to answer," her aunt replied. "Even today people are always talking about war. I agree with you that war is bad."

On their way home Aunt Daisy talked more about herbrothers and the fun they used to have when they were children before the war.

"Thank you for taking me to the service, Aunt Daisy," Annette said when they arrived home. "I will not forget about your uncles and why we keep Remembrance Day."

**3
Annette's
People:
Challenging
the Future**

12 Famous Metis

"Dad, are you famous?" asked Annette one night after supper.

"Whatever made you ask that question," Mr. McKay inquired.

"Fran's uncle is the mayor of a town and Fran says that he is famous," Annette replied.

"What do you think 'famous' means," asked her Mom.

"It means that you are noticed by people and ... that you have a lot of money ... and that you get on TV," Annette replied.

"A famous person may be all those things but that doesn't make someone famous. When you're famous many people will know about you because you have done something important, something many people think is great," Mrs. McKay explained.

"Your school is named after Vincent Massey. He was a famous **Governor-General** of Canada," she continued.

"Some people are famous in a city while others may be famous in the whole country," Mr. McKay added. "People like the Queen are famous in the whole world."

"Do we have any famous Metis people in our city?" asked Annette.

"Yes, we do," answered her mom. "Alderman Lee Anderson has been a member of the **City Council** for many years. You can see his picture in the newspaper quite often."

"I would like to talk to him sometime," Annette said.

"I have an idea," suggested Dad. "We really should make a visit to our city hall. Let's phone Mr. Anderson and ask him if he will give us a tour and tell us about public life."

Annette's Mom and Dad picked her up after school and they drove to City Hall.

"Oh yes, let's do that," begged Annette.

The following Wednesday, Annette's mom and dad picked her up after school and drove to City Hall.

"Hello to the McKay family," Mr. Anderson greeted them. "Welcome to City Hall. You must be Annette," he said as he reached out to shake her hand.

"Yes, I'm Annette," she answered. "Thank you for giving us this tour. We're looking forward to it."

"I'm sure I will enjoy it too," said Mr. Anderson. "I think our large glass and brick city hall is an interesting place. Because it is on the bank of the **South Saskatchewan River**, the large glass windows let people get a beautiful view of nature."

Mr. Anderson explained many things to them as they walked through the building. When they reached the large council chamber, he told Annette she could sit in his chair while her Mom took her picture.

"What do you do when you meet in this big chamber?" Annette wanted to know. "What makes your meetings so important?"

68

He told Annette she could sit in his chair.

"The **mayor** and **council** of the city are the people who make the laws and decide what things to do in order to make life in our city better for people," answered Mr. Anderson.

"That sounds important," said Annette. "How did you get to be a member of city council?"

"Every three years the city has an **election**," answered Mr. Anderson. "The people of the city vote for one person to be the mayor of the city. They also vote for the persons they want to be their leaders on City Council. I was elected and that's how I got to be on the council."

"Did you want to be a leader when you were my age?" asked Annette.

"Yes, Annette. You ask many good questions. Would you like to come to my office so we can talk some more about that?" offered Mr. Anderson.

When they were all seated in Mr. Anderson's office, he told them that even as a young boy he had wanted to be a part of government. In high school he had been president of the student council. Later, he had been asked to help with a Native housing project in central Alberta. He had even tried to get elected to the **Parliament** of Canada once, but wasn't successful.

"And now you are famous, at least in our city, aren't you," Annette asked as she looked up at Mr. Anderson with shiny eyes.

"Not famous, but useful to my community, I hope," he replied.

"My mom said that you are Metis. Are you?" asked Annette.

"Yes," answered Mr. Anderson. "Both my mother and father were Metis who grew up in this area. In fact, my grandfather was a McKay. Perhaps we are related!" he smiled at Annette.

"Ever since I found out that I am Metis, I have learned so much about who my people are. It seems that they are good Canadians just like everyone else. Some are poor and some are rich. Some are famous and some aren't." Annette talked on. "Are there any other famous Metis people?"

"Yes, my dear, there are many," answered Mr. Anderson. "Mr. John Norquay was Metis. He was the **Premier** of Manitoba for ten years back in the 1880s. I'm sure you've heard of Louis Riel, the famous Metis leader in Saskatchewan and Manitoba. His people elected him to the Parliament of Canada twice. Later, he was hanged for his actions against the government. I believe that he was innocent. I have asked the Government of Canada to declare him innocent even though he is dead. If this were done, the story in our history books would have to be changed."

"Mr. John Norquay was Metis."

"I'm sure you've heard of Louis Riel, the famous Metis leader in Saskatchewan and Manitoba."

70

"You may have heard of Brian Trottier, the hockey star."

"Are only **politicians** famous?" asked Annette. "My brother Duncan likes sports. Could he become famous in sports?"

"Well," smiled Mr. Anderson, "I guess that I was a little one-sided. Yes, there are Metis people who are well known in sports. You may have heard of Brian Trottier, the hockey star."

"Yes, I have," replied Annette, "I know that my brother will know all about him."

"Another well known Metis is Douglas Cardinal," continued Mr. Anderson. "He is an **architect** who has designed several

"Another well known Metis is Douglas Cardinal."

71

important buildings in Alberta. He is also the designer of the new Museum of Civilization in Ottawa."

"So far, you've only told me about Metis men. Are Metis women famous too?" asked Annette.

"Yes, a very famous Canadian poet, Pauline Johnston, was of Indian ancestry, said Mr. Anderson. "Perhaps you have read one of her poems, *The Song My Paddle Sings*, in school. Tantoo Cardinal is a famous Canadian movie actress. Maria Campbell is a well known Canadian writer. A few years ago she wrote a book about how she grew up in a Metis community. It is a very interesting story and one you should read soon. It will help you to understand how much our people care about their families. It will also tell you how unkind some people can be in how they treat others."

"Some of the kids at school tease me sometimes," Annette said thoughtfully.

"That's the way some people are, even in this free and beautiful country of Canada," replied Mr. Anderson.

"However, you were right when you said that Metis people are good Canadians. If all of us work hard and honestly, we can make Canada a better place for everyone. But if we are careless about ourselves and others, this will bring harm. I am sure that you are going to be a famous Canadian when you grow up, Annette. Just be sure to keep on caring," Mr. Anderson concluded.

"I think I'm going to be a politician," Annette said as the McKays stood to leave.

"I'm sure you will be a good one if that is what you decide to be, Annette," Mr. Anderson replied.

The Song My Paddle Sings

West wind, blow from your prairie nest,
Blow from the mountains, blow from the west,
The sail is idle, the sailor too;
O wind of the west, we wait for you!
Blow, blow,
I have wooed you so,
But never a favor you bestow.
You rock your cradle the hills between
But scorn to notice my white lateen.

I stow the sail, unship the mast;
I wooed you long, but my wooing's past;
My paddle will lull you into rest.
O drowsy wind of the drowsy west,
Sleep, sleep,
By your mountain steep,
Now fold in slumber your laggard wings,
For soft is the song my paddle sings.

August is laughing across the sky,
Laughing while paddle, canoe and I
Drift, drift,
Where the hills uplift
On either side of the current swift.

The river rolls in its rocky bed;
My paddle is plying its way ahead;
Dip, dip,
While the waters flip
In foam as over their breast we slip.
And oh, the river runs swifter now,
The eddies swirl about my bow!
Swirl, swirl,
How the ripples curl
In many a dangerous pool awhirl!

And forward far the rapids roar,
Fretting their margin for evermore.
Dash, dash,
With a mighty crash,
They seeth , and boil, and bound, and spash.

Be strong, O paddle! be brave, canoe!
The reckless waves you must plunge into.
Reel, reel,
On your trembling keel, —
But never a fear my craft will feel.
We've raced the rapid, we're far ahead!
The river slips through its silent bed,
Sway, sway,
As the bubbles spray
And fall in tinkling tunes away.

And up on the hills against the sky,
A fir tree, rocking its lullaby,
Swings, swings,
Its emerald wings,
Swelling the song that my paddle sings.

— Pauline Johnston

13 A Visit to the Oilfield

"Good morning," Mrs. McKay called up the stairs to wake Annette. "It's time to get ready."

Annette sat up in bed and looked around. "Get ready for what?" she asked sleepily.

"Have you forgotten about your trip to the oil rig with Harvey Cardinal?" her Mom replied.

Annette had forgotten. Now she bounced out of bed and hurriedly got herself ready. When she came down for breakfast she was neatly dressed with her hair brushed.

"You have plenty of time to eat," said her Mom. "Mr. Cardinal isn't coming until 9:30. Your trip will take most of the day. You should get the right start with a good breakfast."

"I'm going with you," Duncan announced. "I want to see if I can get a job on the drilling rig after I finish school."

"Good," smiled Annette. "Then you'll be able to take me on tours by yourself."

"I'll chase you up the **derrick**," Duncan teased her.

Annette was really very happy to have her big brother with her. Both Duncan and Annette were ready by the time Mr. Cardinal drove up to their house.

"Hi, kids," greeted Mr. Cardinal. "Are you ready for the big tour?"

"Hello, Mr. Cardinal," said Annette. "Yes we are. I'm very excited too."

"I'm glad," replied Mr. Cardinal. "I'll make sure that you enjoy yourselves."

"Hi, kids," greeted Mr. Cardinal. *"Are you ready for the big tour?"*

They climbed into Mr. Cardinal's truck and drove out to a drilling rig. Mr. Cardinal explained that this was a "two-stand rig." This meant that it could only drill a hole 1000 metres deep. The larger "three-stand" rigs could drill holes 3,000 metres deep.

"Who is that man on top of the rig," Annette asked.

"That is the **derrick man**," explained Mr. Cardinal. "His job is to line up the next length of pipe with the one already in the drilling hole."

"The men around the bottom of the rig are called **roughnecks**," guessed Duncan.

"That's right," Mr. Cardinal said.

"How do they drill down?" Duncan asked.

"The men around the bottom of the rig are called roughnecks," guessed Duncan.

76

"I'll show you a **drilling bit**," answered Mr. Cardinal. They got out of the truck and walked closer to the drilling rig. Mr. Cardinal picked up a worn drilling bit that was lying on the ground. "This bit is attached to the first length of pipe in the hole," he said. "The diesel motor turns the pipe with the drill bit at the bottom. It cuts through layers of rock deeper down."

"Why are there large banks of dirt around the drilling rig?" asked Annette.

"Before the oil men start drilling, the **site** has to be

"How do they drill down?" Duncan asked.

made ready," Mr. Cardinal said. First the dirt is pushed up into banks. Then the **flare pit** is built. It is used to burn off gas from the well when the pressure is too high. Next the **sump pit** is built. It holds the oil in case the well suddenly blows the oil to the surface."

"What do they do with the well when they are finished drilling?" asked Duncan.

"The well is **capped** until they need the oil or gas it produces," Mr. Cardinal replied.

"Do they just leave the dirt around the well when they are finished?" Annette inquired.

"No," replied Mr. Cardinal. "The dirt is spread around and leveled. Then the area is seeded with grass. Soon the site will look like it did before the drilling started."

On the way back home, Duncan asked Mr. Cardinal how to get a job with the oil company.

"Do they just leave the dirt around the well when they are finished?" Annette inquired.

"You have to go to the employment office and apply for a job," Mr. Cardinal answered. "Most of the major oil companies have Native employment programs. These programs give information to young Indian and Metis people and help them get a job. I'm in charge of my company's Native employment program here. You can come to see me if you want a job in the **oil patch**," he concluded.

"What kinds of jobs could a Metis have in an oil company," asked Annette.

"Any job that is available. The person just has to be willing to work hard and learn," answered Mr. Cardinal.

Soon they arrived back at the McKay's home. Duncan and Annette thanked Mr. Cardinal for the exciting tour.

"Be sure to come and see me when you are ready to become oil workers," Mr. Cardinal told them.

"Oil work looks very interesting. But I want to be a city mayor when I grow up," Annette said with a grin.

"I wish you good luck," smiled Mr. Cardinal as he drove away.

78

14 Ice Fishing

One weekend in February, Mr. McKay and Duncan decided to go fishing at **Reesor Lake**. On Friday evening they got all their equipment together. Duncan had bought some **smelts** for **bait** at the store. Mr. McKay got a can of kernel corn from the kitchen. He knew that trout like corn.

"How can you fish when the water is frozen?" Annette asked at the breakfast table the next morning.

"When lakes freeze over fishermen drill holes in the ice with an **ice auger**," Mr. McKay answered. "They put their baited hooks on fishing lines and drop them down into the water through the holes. Then they wait for a fish to bite! Lake trout, northern pike, pickerel and whitefish are caught this way."

"Doesn't it get too cold?" Annette said with a shiver.

"We are taking an **ice fishing hut** with us," her Dad said. "These huts are placed over the hole to protect the people from chilly winds. In times past, many Metis people fished for food in the winter and summer. Today fishing is usually a sport."

"May I go with you," Annette asked.

"It could be cold out on the open lake even inside the hut," her Dad replied. "You'll have to dress warmly."

"I could sit in the truck to warm up if I have to. Please let me go along," she pleaded.

"If you fall in the hole a fish might gobble you up," teased Duncan.

"Dad, please let me go. I can stay warm, and besides, I can help you drill the hole," Annette persisted.

"You really want to go, don't you," her Dad said. "Alright, get dressed. I'll make an extra sandwich and some hot chocolate for you."

Mr. McKay had borrowed their neighbour's truck for the trip to Reesor Lake. They had a small hut on the back in which to sit while they were fishing.

As they drove along Mr. McKay pointed out some interesting places. Just outside of Medicine Hat the Trans Canada Highway crossed a wide valley.

"That's an old river bed. It is good farming and ranching land now," explained Mr. McKay.

"Where's the water," Annette asked. "How do you know that it is an old river bed?"

"The water was there many thousands of years ago," explained Duncan. He had learned about it in his geography class at school. "During the Ice Age much of this land was under ice," he continued. "Later the weather got warmer and the ice melted, forming a river here. When it was all melted, the river dried up."

Soon they were driving toward the Cypress Hills. The land was covered with snow. The bright sun made it sparkle. Mr. McKay put on his sunglasses to protect his eyes from the glare of the snow.

"I hope that the fish are biting," said Duncan. "Trout from cold water taste extra good. Maybe we can fry some on our camp stove."

"Some people do that but I prefer to have them fried in butter and eat them at home with Mom," was his father's reply.

Soon they arrived at Reesor Lake. Annette could see it from the viewpoint at the top of the hill.

"I'll drill the holes," said Duncan as soon as they reached the spot where they would fish. Annette had to jump up and down to keep warm while Duncan drilled.

Drilling the holes was hard work. The ice was more than fifty centimetres thick! It took Duncan and Annette about ten

"I can see down into the water," exclaimed Annette as she looked into the hole."
"There's a fish down there!"

minutes to hit water. When the first hole was ready, Mr. McKay put the hut over it. Annette was the first to go in.

"I can see down into the water," exclaimed Annette as she looked into the hole. "There's a fish down there!"

"Shh, you'll scare the fish away if you are not quiet," Duncan warned. There was a bench on each side of the hut and Duncan and Annettte sat down. Duncan baited his hook and bobbed it up and down about two metres below the ice. Annette watched closely.

"Look, look," she whispered, it's going after your hook. You got it!" she shouted as the fish grabbed Duncan's hook. Duncan pulled his line up quickly, opened the door of the hut and threw the fish out onto the ice.

"A nice trout," said Dad as he walked over to see it. The fish flopped around on the ice for awhile. Then Mr. McKay put it in a plastic bag.

Duncan put some more bait on the line and then let Annette hold it. "Don't let go when the fish grabs the line," he cautioned her.

81

"I won't," Annette replied as she lowered the hook into the water. Suddenly she felt a tug on the line.

"I've got one," she shouted. Annette pulled it out of the water just like her cousin Joey had shown her last summer. By three o'clock Annette and Duncan had caught enough trout for two suppers. "It's time to start for home," their father called out. "Let's go."

When they reached the top of the Reesor hill, Mr. McKay pointed to the southwest. A long, arched cloud stretched across the sky. "That is a **chinook arch**," he explained. "It means we are going to get warmer weather soon. I just hope the wind doesn't start blowing too hard before we get home."

By the time they reached Elkwater the wind was blowing very strongly. Snow was drifting across the highway and it was getting dark.

"Is it serious, Dad?" Duncan asked.

"If the wind gets any stronger we might not get home tonight," was his father's reply. Mr. McKay looked worried as he kept his eyes fixed on the yellow line on the highway.

At times there was so much snow blowing across the road that they had to stop until there was a lull in the wind.

"It's time to start for home."

82

15 The Blizzard

"Keep your eyes open for a farm," their Dad said. "We may have to stop for awhile until the drifting stops."

"This is a real blizzard, isn't it Dad." Annette sounded excited.

"This is a real blizzard, isn't it Dad?" Annette sounded excited.

"There's a farm yard," Duncan called as he pointed to the left.

Mr. McKay was driving very slowly. He turned the truck in at the gate and drove up to the farmhouse. The wind was blowing even harder, and almost blew Annette over as she stepped out of the truck. Her Dad took her hand as they walked up to the door and knocked. A tall man wearing jeans answered the door.

83

"Well, look what the storm blew in," he said as he saw the McKays. "Come on in, it's warm in here. Come over to the fireplace," he said to Annette. "You look cold. What a storm!"

A lady came in from the kitchen . "I'm Alice and this is my husband George," she said. "Welcome to our home. Please, make yourselves comfortable around the fire. It looks pretty grim outside. I hope no one gets stranded on the highway."

"I'm Fred McKay, and these are my children, Annette and Duncan," Mr. McKay said. "We were just on our way home from ice fishing when we got caught in the blizzard. I'm glad we found your house in time."

Annette sat close to her Dad on the couch. The storm blew in gusts and shook the house. The snow was driving against the windows. "It's getting worse," said George as he peered out the window. "I'm worried about our cattle."

"You can't go out there now, George," Alice said. "You could get lost in the blizzard. Anyway, the cows can take care of themselves. They have shelter in the **pasture**."

"Welcome to our home. please, make yourselves comfortable around the fire," she said.

84

"*The ranchers around here lost a lot of cattle,*" George replied.

As the supper hour approached, Mr. McKay began to worry about Mom. They might not be able to make it home. "Don't worry, Fred," Alice said. We have room and food. Perhaps you should phone your wife and let her know you are safe. I'll get supper ready."

"We have some trout in the truck," Duncan piped up. "I'll bring some in if you want to fry them for supper."

"What a treat!" George said, "We love fresh fish."

Duncan brought the fish in from the car while Mr. McKay telephoned home to explain to Mrs. McKay about the storm and that they were safe.

"I remember a winter several years ago," George began when they were seated at the supper table. "The snow was knee deep when the wind came up. The drifts got so high that the kids used them for ski hills. One drift went right up to the side of the barn to the roof! It took us several days to dig out of that one."

"Wow!" exclaimed Annette. "I wish I could have seen that."

"It was fun after the storm for the kids, but the ranchers around here lost a lot of cattle," George replied.

"My father tells the story," Mr. McKay began, "of a bad winter in the late thirties. My Dad and his friend had decided to walk to a neighbour's farm three miles away for an evening of games. The weather was cold but calm when they started out. Then the wind began to blow when they had walked about half of the distance. Soon they found themselves caught in a swirling blizzard of snow. The wind was blowing from behind them.

"They began to worry about getting lost. Neither of them had a watch and they didn't know how long they had been walking. My Dad stopped and said he needed a rest. His buddy said that if they didn't keep on going, they might not make it alive. He thought that they were close to the farm. But they had lost their way and were stumbling along out on the open prairie."

"They had lost their way and were stumbling along out on the open prairie."

Mr. McKay continued with his story. "Luckily, they came across some **choke cherry** bushes at the edge of a coulee. So they decided to stop and take shelter there. Suddenly, they discovered that they were not alone! Some cows and horses were also looking for shelter from the storm. Some of the cows were lying down in the bushes. My Dad and his buddy each found a cow that was lying down and they lay down beside them on the sheltered side. The cows didn't seem to mind the men pressing close to their warm bodies for protection.

86

"By dawn the next morning, the wind was quite warm and the drifting had stopped. It was a real Chinook and the snow was starting to melt. Since they had walked with the wind the night before, they decided to walk the other direction. They arrived home around noon."

"Am I ever glad we found your farm," Annette said to Alice. "I would hate to spend the night with cows in a storm like this."

It was time to go to bed and soon everyone was fast asleep. The next morning dawned bright and clear. The blizzard had been bad. When Annette looked out the window she saw huge snowdrifts piled against the house.

After breakfast George went outside to start his tractor. Using the scoop on the front, he began to clear the driveway and to pile up the snow. By ten o'clock a snowplow came by the farm clearing the highway. Mr. McKay thanked George and Alice for taking care of them. He offered to pay them some money.

"We had a great time visiting with you. Why should you pay us for that?" George said as he refused the money. "Have a safe trip home."

By ten o'clock a snowplow came by.

By noon the McKays were home again. Mrs. McKay had been waiting anxiously for them.

"Did we ever have an exciting adventure, Mom," Annette said. "You should have heard the stories. I'm glad I went along. And guess what! I caught a fish!"

"Speaking of fish," said Mrs. McKay, "Bring them in, Duncan. We can have fresh fried trout for lunch."

"Did we ever have an exciting adventure, Mom," Annette said.

16 A Social Evening

A loud cheer went up from the crowd. The Metis fiddlers began to play the lively Red River jig.

Annette and Lucy had agreed to pick up Fran for the Metis Fun Night at the community centre. The whole family would be there.

As the girls entered the hall they saw that several people were already there. Soon more and more people began to arrive. Suddenly the announcer stepped up to the **microphone**. "Ladies and gentlemen...," he called out. "Welcome to our Metis Fun Night. Our musicians are ready to play for those who want to dance. Refreshments will be served later. Now all of you be sure to have a good time."

A loud cheer went up from the crowd. The Metis **fiddlers** began to play the lively **Red River Jig**. Couples began to whirl around the floor. The three girls clapped their hands and tapped their feet to the rhythm of the music. Soon Duncan came over to where they were standing.

"May I have this dance?" he asked Fran, and held out his hand. They joined the other dancers on the floor.

A handsome boy came over and asked Annette to dance. Soon Lucy also had a partner and all three girls were whirling about the floor in lively fashion.

After awhile, some refreshments were brought out. Annette saw Tracey Quesnelle and called her over to join them. She introduced Tracey to her friends.

"I'm glad you're here, Tracey," Annette said. "How is college?"

"It's great, but I have to study too hard!" Tracey replied.

"What are you going to be when you are finished?" Annette wanted to know.

"I might be a teacher or a social worker," she replied. "I really like working with kids."

"We'd like you to be *our* teacher," Annette said. Fran and Lucy nodded in agreement.

Tracey's father, Terry Quesnelle, was the announcer. Annette and her friends sat at a table with the McKay and Quesnelle families.

"We'd like you to be our teacher," Annette said.

90

"Did you know that the Quesnelle family was one of the first pioneer families in this area?" Mrs. McKay asked Annette.

"That's right," Mr. Quesnelle said. "My grand-father was Michel Quesnelle. He came to Medicine Hat from **Wyoming** in 1875. He became a scout for the Northwest Mounted Police. Later, he ranched east of here. It is said that he was one of the best **ropers** in the world."

"I'd like to study science and become an engineer," Duncan said.

"I hear that you are back at school, Terry," said Mr. McKay to Mr. Quesnelle. "What are your plans?"

"I haven't been able to drive trucks since I hurt my back," Mr. Quesnelle replied. "I'm back in school to get a better education. Perhaps I can get a better job working with people when I'm finished."

"Tracey wants to be a teacher like you, Mom," said Annette. She was looking at Tracey with admiration. "I think she will be a good teacher, don't you, Dad?"

"Good for you, Tracey," said Mr. McKay. "Yes, I think she will be a very good teacher."

"I think I would like to go to university after high school. I'd like to study science and become an engineer," Duncan said. "Ever since Mr. Cardinal took us out to the oil field I've been thinking about getting a job there. People will always need oil and the things they make from it."

"I'm going to be a politician," Annette said. "Then I'll be famous!"

"I'm glad we all have the chance to try for the jobs we want," Tracey said.

"I'm glad we all have the chance to try for the jobs we want," Tracey said. "In fact, we can choose to do other jobs if we aren't happy with our first choice. I changed my mind a few times before I decided to be a teacher. *If we do well at school, we will have more choices about what we want to do later. After all, education is the key to our future.*"

"Quite often the Metis part of us has to stay hidden in school," said Duncan. "There are times when we feel that we don't really belong. I felt like that when I was in junior high school. Now that I'm in high school, I don't feel that way anymore. I wonder why."

"I know how you felt," said Tracey "Maybe it is because we are too worried about what others might think of us."

"I'm proud to be Metis," Annette said to her friends. "There are over 500 of us in Medicine Hat. Metis people are just as good as anyone else. We should just keep doing the best we can."

"That's right, Annette," Mr. McKay replied proudly. "The best future for us is to be proud of who we are and plan to be successful."

"All Metis people need to understand that," added Mr. Quesnelle. "Other people will respect us if we feel strong inside about ourselves. Remember Louis Riel? Just before he died he said, 'In a hundred years my people will rise again'. It is now over a hundred years later. Our people are rising again by becoming educated and strong."

After the musicians had rested, one of them picked up his guitar and walked to the microphone. "Ladies and gentlemen," he announced. "Let's sing a few songs together."

He strummed his guitar and everyone started to sing. They sang loud, lively songs that made everyone happy. They also sang soft, sad songs that almost made Annette want to cry. Annette and her friends got up and moved closer to the stage.

"What is he wearing?" Lucy whispered to Annette. He looked like he was wearing a long scarf around his waist.

"That is part of the **traditional** Metis clothing," Annette replied. "It's called a **sash**. My father says it is what the early French fur traders wore."

Other men were wearing mukluks and beaded shirts with **bandanas** around their necks. They looked so handsome in their traditional clothes.

Mr. Cardinal came over to where Annette and her friends were sitting. "Are you having a good time?" he asked.

"That is part of the traditional Metis clothing," Annette replied.

93

"You can see that our people really know how to have a good time," he said. "In the past, Metis people would take turns holding these dances in their homes. They would move the furniture outside to make room for the dancers. Sometimes life was so hard that they couldn't buy fiddles. Then the fiddlers would make their own. You can't have a dance without a fiddle!" he laughed.

"I love those fiddlers," Lucy said. "They can make our toes tap without even trying."

"Metis fiddlers are among the best in the world," said Mr. Cardinal. "They can make a fiddle cry or laugh if they are in the mood. Many Metis fiddlers taught themselves to play without ever taking lessons."

"We have other artists too," added Annette. "You saw the fancy clothes some of us are wearing tonight. Making fancy clothes is also a Metis tradition. We have great Metis painters and writers too. Some day I hope other people will notice how good they are."

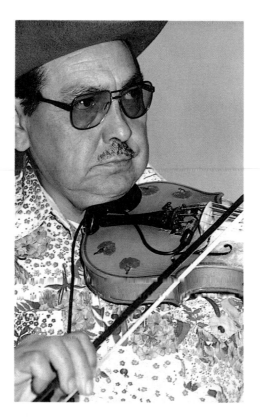

"I'm glad you had a good time," Mr. Cardinal said. "We want all Canadians to know about Metis people and our good times. I hope that we will see you again."

Tracey agreed to take the three girls home. After they said good night to Fran and Lucy, Annette told Tracey about her dream about the Indian woman who had told her to learn about her ancestors.

"I love those fiddlers," Lucy said. *"They can make our toes tap without even trying."*

94

"What can I learn from the Indians?" Annette asked her friend.

"What can I learn from the Indians?" Annette asked her friend. "How will it help me when I grow up?"

"My Dad has some Indian friends," Tracey answered. "They could help you. My Dad told me that the Indians took things from nature as a gift from the Great Spirit. They thought that they should take care of nature.

"I think some people take more from nature than they need," she continued. "If people keep doing that we will all be much poorer. That is one lesson we can learn from our Indian ancestors."

"Does that mean that we should all go back to living in tipis and hunting?" Annette asked.

"I don't think so," Tracey replied. "It is more important that we try not to waste the things we have now. People should make sure that when they cut a tree down they plant another one. Our wild animals and birds should be protected too."

"That sounds like a good idea, Tracey," Annette said. "I'll try to remember what you have told me."

Annette fell asleep as soon as her head hit the pillow. As she drifted off to sleep she began to dream. The same Indian woman who had talked to her before stood beside her bed.

The Indian woman smiled at her. "You are learning well, my daughter," she said. "Kindness and friendship are a part of your people's **heritage**. The knowledge you gain now will help you in the future. "Then she faded away and Annette slept soundly.

The Indian woman smiled at her. *"You are learning well, my daughter,"* she said.

Glossary

Glossary

Adaptable The ability to change to meet new or different circumstances.

Agent Someone who buys or sells goods for another person.

Altitude The height of the land above sea level or the height of anything above the ground.

Ancestors The people from whom we and our parents are descended. A **great-grandmother** is an ancestor.

Archaeologist A person who studies a people's past, including looking at the remains of their houses, tools, clothing and other things they used.

Architect A person who makes plans for buildings and houses.

Artifacts Things such as tools, dishes or clothing that were made by people long ago.

Auction A sale at which things such as furs are sold to the person who bids the most money.

Bait Food or other things such as worms which are used to catch fish

(Indian)Band A group of Indian families who live together on a **reserve**.

Bandana A colourful piece of cloth worn around the neck. Early French fur traders and cowboys wore them.

Bannock A kind of bread or biscuit made from flour, lard and water. It was used by Native people and early settlers.

Beast Another name for an animal.

Blackfoot Indians A tribe of **Indian** people who lived on the prairies of Alberta and Montana. One of their reserves is at Gleichen, Alberta.

Blizzard A blinding snow storm.

Bungalow A one-story house.

Canadian Legion A club for the men and women who have served in Canada's armed forces.

Capped A capped oil well is one that has been closed until the oil or gas is needed.

Career The work people choose to do for most of their lives.

Cenotaph A statue or monument built in memory of soldiers who died in a war.

Chinook A warm, dry wind that blows over the Rocky Mountains from the Pacific Ocean. When it reaches the prairies it melts the snow and brings warm temperatures.

Chinook arch The band of cloud that forms an arch over the western horizon when a chinook wind is blowing.

Choke cherry A small tree or shrub with dark red berries.

City Council The group of people who are elected to run a city.

Conductor The person in charge of a train.

Constable A police officer.

Coulee A valley on the prairies made by water or wind wearing down the soil. Often the sides are quite steep.

Cree Indians A tribe of **Indians** who live in the northern prairies and forests of Alberta, Saskatchewan and Manitoba. Cree Indians also live in Ontario and Quebec.

Curator A person who is in charge of a museum.

Derrick A portable steel tower used for drilling oil and gas wells. It is also called a drilling rig.

Derrick man The person who works at the top of an oil drilling rig. This person guides the drilling pipes when they are joined together.

Dictatorship A kind of government where one person rules over everyone else and there are no elections.

(The) Dirty Thirties A term used to describe the dusty conditions on the prairies during the dry years between 1930 and 1939. It is another name for **The Great Depression**.

Dome Car A kind of railway car with a high glass roof and big windows on top.

Donkey pumps The bobbing pumps over an oil well that bring oil out of the ground and into a pipeline or tank.

Drilling Bit The steel tool used to drill into the ground for an oil well.

Election When the people of a community, a province or a country vote to decide who will be their leaders.

Elk A large member of the deer family.

Embroidery Fancy needlework patterns sewn on cloth or leather clothing to decorate them.

Employment When people work to earn a living.

Europeans People who live in or came from Europe.

Explorers People who travel to places where no one else from their land has ever been.

Extinct Something that once was alive but no longer exists.

Fertilizer Chemicals that help plants grow better.

Fiddlers People who play the violin.

Flare pit A pit dug near an oil well to burn off gas that sometimes comes up ahead of the oil.

Flour Mill A place where wheat is ground into flour.

Fur Trader A person who buys or sells animal furs.

Geography The study of the earth and different countries.

Goods Things that are made for sale.

Governor General The representative of the Queen in Canada.

(The) Great Depression The time between 1929 and 1939 when many people were out of work and had little money. It is called The Great Depression because it happened in many countries.

Great-Grandfather Your grandmother or grandfather's father.

Great-Grandmother Your grandmother or grandfather's mother.

Gun Ports Spaces in the walls of a fort through which cannons or other guns could be pointed.

Hardship Something that is difficult or very hard for a person.

Heritage The language and **traditions** that are part of a person's culture.

History The story of how people lived and what they did in the past.

Hivernant The name some Metis were called who traveled around in the summer to hunt and settled in villages in the winter.

Horizon The place where the sky and the land seem to meet when you look into the distance.

Ice Age A period, millions of years ago, when the earth was covered with ice.

Ice auger A drill used to make a hole in the ice for fishing.

Ice fishing hut A small, portable building used to keep warm by people who are ice fishing.

Identity The things that make up a person like how they look, their habits and their history.

Immigrant A person who comes to live in one country from another country.

Indian The name Columbus gave to the people he met when he found North America. They are the people who lived in North America before the settlers came.

Industry The work of people producing food or goods for a living. Also the term used to describe some businesses .

Inherited What those things are that a person gets from their parents or their ancestors.

Invaded When one country is attacked by another country's army.

Kikino A **Cree** word meaning home.

(The) Last Post The last song played at **Remembrance Day** ceremonies and at the funerals of soldiers.

Legislature The building in which the government of the province meets.

Lifestyle The way a person lives including the food they eat, the music they listen to, the things they do for fun.

Mass The words a **priest** says and the music at a Catholic church service.

Massacre When a lot of people are killed for no reason.

Mayor The chief elected leader in a town or city.

Memorial service A sevice held to remember a person or people who died. A memorial service is held each November 11 to remember the soldiers who died in the wars.

Metis The people who have both Indian and European ancestors. It comes from a French word that means "mixed blood."

Microphone A device that people speak into to make their voices sound louder.

Moccasins Soft leather shoes without a heel.

Moose A large animal as big as a horse with broad horns that lives in the forests and mountains.

Mukluks Footwear that come up above the ankles. They are made from animal skins. Sometimes they are embroidered.

Museum A building where important artifacts and pictures are kept.

Native Someone whose ancestors have lived in a land for many generations. **Indian** and **Metis** people are sometimes called Natives of North America.

Nazi The name given to the **dictatorship** which ran Germany from 1933 to 1945.

Nomadic When people move around often rather than staying in one community.

Northern pike A kind of fish which lives in lakes and rivers in North America.

Northwest Mounted Police
The early name for the Royal Canadian Mounted Police.

Oil patch The name oil workers call the area where they are drilling and have found oil. It is also another name for the oil industry.

Panorama Another name for all the scenery around you, or everything you can see.

Parliament The name given to the group of men and women who are elected to run the government of Canada and help make the laws that we obey.

Pasture A field on a farm or ranch where cattle or horses graze.

Pemmican A food made from berries, fat and dried meat. It was stored in bags made from animal skins and would not spoil for a long time.

Politician Someone who tries to get elected to government. Members of **City Council**, the **Legislature** and **Parliament** are politicians.

Poppies Red flowers sometimes made from paper which people wear on **Remembrance Day** in honour of soldiers who died in the wars.

Premier The leader of the government of a province. He is a member of the **Legislature**.

Priest The minister of a church.

Prosper To be successful.

Rebellion When people don't like the government and try to change it. Sometimes they try to use force to change the government.

Red River Cart A two wheeled cart used by the **Metis** and early settlers to move things before the railroad was built. The wooden wheels were as high as a person. The cart was often pulled by oxen.

Red River Jig A lively dance done by the **Metis** similar to square dancing.

Remembrance Day November 11. The day set aside to remember the men and women who fought in **World Wars I and II**.

(Indian) Reserve Land set aside by the government just for **Indians** to live on.

Room and Board A term used to describe the cost of rent and food.

Roper A cowboy who uses a rope to catch calves and steers.

Roughneck A worker who works on an oil drilling rig.

Sash A colourful piece of cloth that Metis people used to wear around their waists.

Saskatoon berries Small berries like blueberries that grow on bushes in the shady parts of **coulees** on the prairies.

Schooner A sailing ship used long ago. It had two or more masts to hold the sails up in the wind.

Shawl A piece of clothing worn to cover the shoulders.

Sioux Indians A tribe of **Indians** living in the western United States.

Site A place where something is located or where something happened.

Smelt A small fish used for food or for bait to catch other fish.

Soup kitchen A place in a city where hungry people could get something to eat. Often they got a bowl of soup and a piece of bread.

Squatter A person who builds a home without permission on land they don't own.

Stock inspector Someone who inspects farm animals for diseases.

Sump pit A large pit dug near an oil well to catch the oil if it gushes up from the drilled hole before the well is **capped**.

Tipi The home that **Indian** people lived in long ago.

Trader A person who exchanges one kind of thing for another. In earlier times **fur traders** exchanged guns, axes and other things for the furs trapped by **Indian** and **Metis** people.

Trading post The building where a trader stored his goods and where the trading took place.

Tradition The special ways that a people did things. They include the habits and ways of doing things that children inherit from their parents.

Trainman The person who works on a train as the **conductor's** helper.

Trap line The area set aside for a trapper to set out his traps for animals.

Unemployment When people don't have a job.

Unemployment Insurance Commission The part of government that pays people who do not have a job.

Upwind The direction from the which the wind is blowing.

Venison The meat of the deer used for food.

ViaRail The passenger train that takes people across Canada.

Wages The money a person is paid for working.

Whiskey A strong drink made from grain.

World War I A war between many nations which began in 1914 and ended in 1919. Canada took sides with Britain against Germany and Austria. Many Canadian soldiers fought and died. We remember them on **Remembrance Day**.

World War II A war between **Nazi** Germany and many other countries which began in 1939 and ended in 1945. Again, many Canadian soldiers fought in this war. We remember them on **Remembrance Day**.

Photocredits

Plains Publishing gratefully acknowledges the assistance and cooperation of the following individuals, agencies and corporations in providing the visual materials used in this book. Credits are by page number, coded as follows:
T - top; B - bottom; R - right; L - left; GAI: Glenbow-Alberta Institute; PAA: Provincial Archives of Alberta; PAB: Public Affairs Bureau.

Cover: Red River cart: William Pearce Collection, courtesy University of Alberta Archives; Metis home: Henry Julien in *L'Opinion Publique*, 8 Oct., 1874, courtesy GAI (NA-47-11); Metis horseman: Henry Kalen, courtesy Manitoba Museum of Man and Nature; Louis Riel: Fred Russell, courtesy GAI (NA-635-1); Metis soldiers: M. Poitras, courtesy GAI (NA-4712-1); Blanche McDonald: courtesy Blanche McDonald Institute; Brian Trottier: courtesy Bruce Bennett.

7 Brady Collection, courtesy GAI (PA-2218-985)
11 courtesy Medicine Hat Museum (PC1950)
12 L: *Harper's Monthly*, Oct., 1860, courtesy GAI (NA-1406-7); R: *Picturesque Canada*, ca. 1882, courtesy GAI (NA-1041-4)
13 courtesy Peter Mueller
15 courtesy Minnesota Historical Society
23 courtesy Travel Alberta
24 courtesy Dan Buffalo
25 courtesy Travel Alberta
32 courtesy Provincial Museum of Alberta
38 Henry Kalen, courtesy Manitoba Museum of Man and Nature
40 J.J Barrie, courtesy Medicine Hat Museum
41 courtesy Peter Mueller
47 courtesy Peter Mueller
50 courtesy Travel Manitoba
52 William Pearce Collection, courtesy University of Alberta Archives
53 J.M. Mix, 1853, courtesy GAI (NA-1274-2)
56 courtesy PAA (A5665)
57 courtesy GAI (ND3-6523a)
58 Brady Collection, courtesy GAI (PA-2218-985)
59 courtesy Peter Mueller
62 T,B: courtesy Frank Webber, Jr.
63 courtesy Frank Webber, Jr.
64 W.V. Ring, courtesy GAI (NA-2365-86)
68 courtesy Peter Mueller
70 T: courtesy GAI (NA-1816-1); B: Fred Russell, courtesy GAI (NA-2631-2)
71 T: courtesy Bruce Bennett; B: courtesy Douglas Cardinal Architect Ltd.
72 Terry Lusty, courtesy Aboriginal Multi-Media Society of Alberta
76 courtesy Nova, An Alberta Corporation
77 courtesy Alberta Energy Corporation
78 courtesy Nova, An Alberta Company
85 courtesy Browarny Photographics
87 courtesy Public Affairs Bureau
89 Mark McCallum, courtesy Aboriginal Multi-Media Society of Alberta
91 courtesy Public Affairs Bureau
92 TL, BL, BR: courtesy PAB; TR: courtesy Dale Ripley
93 courtesy Alberta Archeological Survey
94 courtesy Aboriginal Multi-Media Society of Alberta
95 courtesy PAB

Other assistance was kindly provided by Travel Saskatchewan, Travel Manitoba, Petroleum Resources Communications Foundation, PetroCanada, The New York Islanders, W.J. (Jack) Elliot, Lynette Walton, Kathy Lipsett, Marlene Witschl, Terry Quesnelle, Doug Leighton, Terry Lusty, Rocky Woodward, Carole Philippe, Gertrude McLaren, Donny White, Ruth King, Vern Modin and Ed Gallup.